true
discipleship

2 CORINTHIANS 1 – 7

by James Hughes

thegoodbook
COMPANY

true discipleship
the good book guide to 2 Corinthians 1 – 7
© James Hughes/The Good Book Company, 2009.
Reprinted 2013

The Good Book Company
Tel (UK): 0333 123 0880
Tel (int): + (44) 208 942 0880
Tel: (US): 866 244 2165
Email: info@thegoodbook.co.uk

Websites
UK: www.thegoodbook.co.uk
N America: www.thegoodbook.com
Australia: www.thegoodbook.com.au
New Zealand: www.thegoodbook.co.nz

ISBN: 9781906334758

Printed in China

CONTENTS

introduction: good book guides

Every Bible-study group is different—yours may take place in a church building, in a home or in a cafe, on a train, over a leisurely mid-morning coffee or squashed into a 30-minute lunch break. Your group may include new Christians, mature Christians, non-Christians, mums and tots, students, businessmen or teens. That's why we've designed these *Good Book Guides* to be flexible for use in many different situations.

Our aim in each session is to uncover the meaning of a passage, and see how it fits into the "big picture" of the Bible. But that can never be the end. We also need to appropriately apply what we have discovered to our lives. Let's take a look at what is included:

⊕ **Talkabout:** Most groups need to "break the ice" at the beginning of a session, and here's the question that will do that. It's designed to get people talking around a subject that will be covered in the course of the Bible study.

⊥ **Investigate:** The Bible text for each session is broken up into manageable chunks, with questions that aim to help you understand what the passage is about. **The Leader's Guide** contains **guidance on questions**, and sometimes ☒ additional "follow-up" questions.

⊡ **Explore more (optional):** These questions will help you connect what you have learned to other parts of the Bible, so you can begin to fit it all together like a jig-saw; or occasionally look at a part of the passage that's not dealt with in detail in the main study.

⊖ **Apply:** As you go through a Bible study, you'll keep coming across **apply** sections. These are questions to get the group discussing what the Bible teaching means in practice for you and your church. ⊡ **Getting personal** is an opportunity for you to think, plan and pray about the changes that you personally may need to make as a result of what you have learned.

⊓ **Pray:**hWe want to encourage prayer that is rooted in God's word—in line with His concerns, purposes and promises. So each session ends with an opportunity to review the truths and challenges highlighted by the Bible study, and turn them into prayers of request and thanksgiving.

The **Leader's Guide** and introduction provide historical background information, explanations of the Bible texts for each session, ideas for **optional extra** activities, and guidance on how best to help people uncover the truths of God's word.

why study 2 Corinthians?

If anyone is in Christ, the new creation has come:
the old has gone, the new is here! All this is from God...
2 Corinthians 5 v 17-18

Many of the problems in our churches today are the same things that
the Corinthians struggled with. Problems with pride and arrogance, with
misunderstanding the gospel, with thinking that the Christian life is more
about health, wealth and happiness than about suffering and persevering
through difficulties to reach glory.

Just like the Corinthians, we get stuck in the here and now, and forget about
eternity. Like them, we are more impressed by fame and fortune than by
faithfulness to Jesus Christ. We too struggle when life gets hard, and would
love life to be a prosperous bed of roses. We would love to be strong, but
know that we are weak—fragile clay pots that are filled with the immense
treasure of God's grace.

So Paul's letter speaks to us as it spoke to them—about the way of true
discipleship. And the reality he paints is not for the faint-hearted. Because it
involves suffering as well as comfort. It means listening to hard truth as well as
receiving and enjoying forgiveness. It involves dying to ourselves and the world,
as well as living for the Lord.

All these issues and much more are covered in this Good Book Guide, where
we'll look at the first seven chapters of 2 Corinthians over nine sessions.
So read on, as together we get to grips with what it means to live as true
disciples—God's "new creation" in the old creation that is passing away.

Acts 18 1-18-

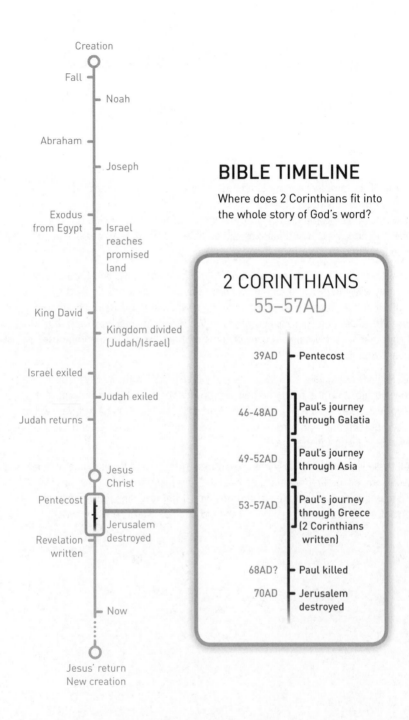

Creation

Fall

Noah

Abraham

Joseph

Exodus
from Egypt

Israel
reaches
promised
land

King David

Kingdom divided
(Judah/Israel)

Israel exiled

Judah exiled

Judah returns

Jesus
Christ

Pentecost

Jerusalem
destroyed

Revelation
written

Now

Jesus' return
New creation

BIBLE TIMELINE

Where does 2 Corinthians fit into
the whole story of God's word?

2 CORINTHIANS
55–57AD

39AD — Pentecost

46-48AD — Paul's journey
through Galatia

49-52AD — Paul's journey
through Asia

53-57AD — Paul's journey
through Greece
(2 Corinthians
written)

68AD? — Paul killed

70AD — Jerusalem
destroyed

1

2 Corinthians 1 v 1-11

SUFFERING AND COMFORT
God's work in our troubles

introduction

> **Read 2 Corinthians 1 v 1-2**

In 2 Corinthians Paul writes to the church in Corinth. It's a church he's close to—he has already written them at least one letter (1 Corinthians) and spent 18 months there (see Acts 18 v 1-18). Paul has already said some challenging things to the Corinthians, and there are more in this letter, but he begins with a greeting.

Notice how Paul writes to the church in Corinth, and also to the holy people / saints (believers) in Achaia. The things he needed to say to the Corinthians would also be relevant for other Christians in a large part of what is now modern-day Greece.

DICTIONARY

Apostle (v 1): someone chosen and sent by Jesus to teach and serve the Christian church.

Holy people / saints (v 1): those who God set apart for himself. Christians.

Achaia (v 1): southern Greece (see map above).

Grace (v 2): God's gift of forgiveness to people who don't deserve it.

As we read 2 Corinthians, we're reading a letter Paul wrote nearly 2,000 years ago. But we are also reading a letter written to us. That's why we're going to spend time seeking to understand it, and applying it to our lives.

⊕ talkabout

1. Think about some of the difficult situations you have faced in life (eg: work, relationships, money, ill-health, failure, disappointments). How do difficulties change people, for better or for worse?

   WHEN THEY LOOK BACK ON A DIFFICULT SITUATION THEY CAN SEE THE LORDS PROJONES. AND DRAW CLOSER TO Him

   • What have you done in the past to cope with difficult situations?

   PRAY. & TRUST

⊕ investigate

❯ Read 2 Corinthians 1 v 3-11

Paul now comes to his first subject—comfort in times of trouble. He wants to share with the Corinthians his experience of God at work.

2. Look at verses 3 and 4. Who comforts who here?

   GOD. & GOD IN US

> **DICTIONARY**
>
> **Christ (v 5):** a title which means "the anointed one". Jesus is God's chosen King, (kings were anointed with oil), who was promised by God to rescue his people.

3. How is God described in verses 3 and 4? What does this tell us about God's relationship to us and his character?

FATHER OF Compassion

⊟ apply

4. What is the worst trouble that you can imagine striking you?

Ill HEALTH.

- How does the possibility of this kind of trouble affect the way you live now?

Try to live more healthy (eat etc)

- How can the phrase "the God of all comfort, who comforts us in all our troubles" (v 3-4) transform your life right now?

No matter how much you are suffering, the Lord is with you.

⊡ getting personal

Of all the troubles that might come to us in this world, there is none that leaves us in a place where God cannot comfort us—totally. Can you trust your compassionate heavenly Father for this? And if you can, have you ever comforted others with this truth about God?

There are two other places in the New Testament where God, the "Father of our Lord Jesus Christ", is praised for who he is and what he has done—read **Ephesians 1 v 3-14** and **1 Peter 1 v 3-5**.

Make one list of words that describe our Father God, and another list of what he has done.

What new insights into God's character have you discovered?

⊡ **investigate**

God reveals himself to us in his word, and here we find out about his perfect fatherly compassion and care for us, most of all in sending his Son for us.

5. What did Christ suffer (v 5)?

> THE WEIGHT OF ALL SIN.
> SEPARATION FROM THE FATHER
> MOCKED & SCOFFED.

6. Why does Paul suffer?

- v 5:
> THE LORD SAID YOU SHALL SUFFER
> FOR MY SAKE.
> THEY HATED ME FIRST.

- v 6:

7. How is Paul comforted (v 4 and 5)?

8. What do Paul and the Corinthians share (v 7)?

➡ apply

9. What troubles have you experienced as a result of being a follower of Jesus Christ?

Fiery DARTS.
Riacure.

• How have you drawn comfort from knowing Jesus as Saviour and Lord?

Phrasm ai

⬇ investigate

10. What was the purpose of Paul's sufferings in Asia (v 8-11)?

11. What should suffering make us do?

Be more compassionate

⤷ apply

12. What will help you to turn to "the God of all comfort" in difficult circumstances?

Knowing his grace is sufficient!

⊡ getting personal

Think about your experience of God's comfort in sufferings. Who, in a similar situation, could you help?

⬆ pray

- Give thanks to God for who he is and what he has done.

- Reflect on how God has helped you through suffering.

- Seek God's guidance as to how you can help others.

- Pray for God's strength in any suffering you or others in the group are currently facing.

Thanks - Ian & Rachel for their farm.
Jim & James move.

2 Corinthians 1 v 12 – 2 v 4
FAITHFUL OR FICKLE?
When plans have to change

The story so far

True disciples of Jesus Christ will see suffering as part of God's plan to help us grow more like Christ.

⊕ talkabout

1. What kind of people do you find it easiest to listen to?

   Humble, gentle

   • How do you think the world around us influences our choice of who we listen to most?

⊕ investigate

❯ Read 2 Corinthians 1 v 12-14: Boasting

2. Why might the Corinthians be reluctant to boast about Paul (v 12-14)?

   Did not fully understand his message.

3. When will they boast about Paul (1 v 14)?

IN THE DAY OF THE LORD!

In verses 12 to 14 we begin to see a little of the "problem" between Paul and the Corinthians. They have "understood ... in part", but Paul wants them to understand fully; he wants them to hear what he has to say, even when he has to say difficult things. Here Paul has to defend his role as an apostle—teaching and declaring God's word to the Corinthians. The following verses show us one reason why Paul's role as an apostle was being questioned.

> **Read 2 Corinthians 1 v 15 – 2 v 4: Travel plans**

4. How might the Corinthians view Paul's change of travel plans (v 15-17)?

5. Paul calls God himself as a witness to his plans (v 18, 23). Why is it such a big deal for Paul to show that his change of plans was not because of worldly fickleness (v 19-22)?

⊕ apply

6. Look again at 1 v 12-14. How should Christian leaders help people to take the good news about Jesus Christ seriously? And how can they hinder that?

- Why is it important for all Christians, leaders or not, to act with holiness, sincerity and grace?

⊡ getting personal

Like Paul, your church leaders and Bible teachers should reflect the faithfulness of God and the gospel of Jesus Christ. How often do you pray for them—to do that in every situation?

And how important is it for you to bring honour to God by your holiness, sincerity and grace?

⊡ explore more

optional

Look at verses 19-22. *Summarise, in a sentence or two, what God has done for the Corinthians (and Christians today).*

How do these truths make our lives different from those around us?

⊕ investigate

7. Why didn't Paul go to Corinth (1 v 23 – 2 v 4)?

In 2 v 3-4 we get another glimpse of Paul's difficult relationship with the Corinthians. He mentions a painful letter he has had to write. This letter is probably not 1 Corinthians, but another one written between 1 and 2 Corinthians, which God has chosen not to preserve for us.

8. Why was Paul's visit going to be painful (2 v 1-4)?

9. What does this section of the letter tell us about Paul?

⊡ explore more

optional

It can be helpful when reading Paul's letters to understand some of the background from the book of Acts. Read **Acts 18 v 1-18**—Paul's first visit to Corinth.

What did Paul do in Corinth (v 1-5)? How might the "day-job" have affected some people's view of Paul?

Paul's ministry was "successful" in Corinth (v 6-8), but it wasn't easy. How did God reassure him (v 9-11)?

What do verses 12 to 17 show us about the relationship between the Jews, Christians and Romans?

How does this passage help us understand Paul's relationship with the Corinthians?

⊡ apply

Many of the Corinthians had a strained relationship with Paul, and his changed travel plans hadn't helped.

10. What might we use as a reason not to listen to someone teaching God's word?

11. How does knowing who God is help us to listen to those who teach his word?

⊡ getting personal

Is there a leader or Bible teacher in your church who you find it hard to listen to? Repent of your wrong attitudes, and ask God to help you to hear his word from them.

⊡ pray

- Pray for wisdom in hearing God's word—that we would listen to what his word says, and not get distracted by the messenger.

- Pray for a greater understanding of who God is and what he has done for us.

- Pray for those in leadership, that they would live and act with sincerity, holiness and grace.

3 TRUTH AND FORGIVENESS

2 Corinthians 2 v 5 – 3 v 6

Speaking out in Christ

The story so far

True disciples of Jesus Christ will see suffering as part of God's plan to help us grow more like Christ.

True disciples of Christ will be willing to hear and receive God's word, and will love and accept the messenger.

⊕ talkabout

1. Think of situations in which you know you should speak out, but find it very difficult to do so.

   Why do you fail to do the right thing?

⊕ investigate

❯ Read 2 Corinthians 2 v 5-11

Paul has outlined why he changed his travel plans and has explained that he didn't want to make another painful visit. Now he turns to two matters. The first concerns the church in Corinth (2 v 5-11), and the second is more personal to Paul, but also has a much wider relevance for all believers (2 v 12-17).

> **DICTIONARY**
>
> **Satan (v 11):** the Hebrew word *satan* means "adversary". Satan, also called the devil, is the adversary of God, his people, and all that is good.

2. Someone has caused grief by his actions. Who did he grieve (2 v 5, 10)?

3. This person has been disciplined. Now Paul calls for forgiveness. Find two reasons why (2 v 6-7, 11).

Notice how Paul leads the way in ensuring that this person is both disciplined and forgiven. Discipline was clearly a painful process—Paul had to pull on all his authority to make it happen (v 9). But now that repentance has taken place, restoration is needed. Discipline and forgiveness are not incompatible opposites—they are both an expression of Paul's care for the Corinthians.

⚬ **explore more**

optional

> ❯ **Read Luke 17 v 1-4**

What does Jesus say about forgiveness in v 3-4?

What do you think the connection is between v 1-2 and 3-4?

⊟ **apply**

4. Why is discipline sometimes so difficult to do—and to accept?

5. Why is forgiveness sometimes so difficult?

• How does this passage help us to be more forgiving?

⊌ investigate

> **▶ Read 2 Corinthians 2 v 12-17**

6. Paul describes himself and other gospel teachers as "the pleasing aroma of Christ" (v 15). What creates this "smell" (v 14)?

7. How do different people respond to the fragrance (v 15-16)?

8. How does Paul feel about his role and how does he approach it (v 16-17)?

❯ Read 2 Corinthians 3 v 1-6

9. Why doesn't Paul need letters of recommendation to the Corinthians (v 1-3)?

DICTIONARY

Spirit (v 3): the Holy Spirit. God sends his Spirit to help people who become Christians.
Covenant (v 6): agreement.

• What was important to some of the Corinthians (v 1)?

• What was important to Paul (2 v 17; 3 v 2-3)?

10. Where does Paul's competence come from (v 4-6)?

⟶ apply

11. How can Paul's perspective on evangelism help us as we talk to others?

In this section we have seen Paul speaking out in a number of ways that could be received as unwelcome—his painful visit (2 v 1); the test of obedience in his difficult letter (2 v 4, 9: probably an instruction to discipline the person who had caused everyone grief, v 5); his urgent plea to the Corinthians to now forgive the repentant sinner (v 8); and his ongoing ministry of teaching the gospel, which, though the fragrance of life to some, is also the smell of death to others.

⊕ investigate

12. Look back at the situations discussed in question 1. How different is Paul in his commitment to speak out as a minister of Christ, both inside and outside the church?

• What explains that difference?

⊡ getting personal

Is there someone you now have confidence to share the gospel with? Use your newly found confidence!

↑ pray

Pray for...

• a willingness to accept discipline and to support your leaders in this.

• the ability to forgive others.

• the confidence to share the good news.

And give thanks to God for what he has done for us in Jesus Christ, which makes all this possible, as the Holy Spirit works in our lives!

2 Corinthians 3 v 7-18

4 THE OLD AND THE NEW
The difference that Christ makes

The story so far

True disciples of Jesus Christ will see suffering as part of God's plan to help us grow more like Christ.

True disciples of Christ will be willing to hear and receive God's word, and will love and accept the messenger.

True disciples speak out for Christ even in the face of difficulties or rejection.

⊕ talkabout

1. When someone mentions "history", what other words come to mind?

   • How similar are your feelings about the Old Testament?

⊕ investigate

❯ Read 2 Corinthians 3 v 7-11

Here Paul begins to talk about the old covenant (God's promises to and agreement with his people in the Old Testament) and compares it with the new covenant (God's promises to and agreement with his people in the New Testament, in Jesus Christ).

> **DICTIONARY**
>
> **Righteousness (v 9):** being right with God, which is only possible through Jesus Christ.

2. Look at how Paul compares the old and new covenants and complete the table.

Old covenant (ministry that brought death)	New covenant (ministry that brings life)
(v 7)	(v 8)
(v 7, 11)	(v 11)
(v 9)	(v 9)
(v 10)	(v 10)

3. What does Paul do in these verses to show us just how amazing the new covenant is?

→ **apply**

The new covenant is better than the old. But Paul's argument can show the surpassing glory of the new covenant only because the old covenant was glorious.

4. How can we remind ourselves of the glory of the old covenant?

- Discuss why people find it difficult to read or learn from the Old Testament. What sort of things can help us to overcome this?

What can you start doing right now to get to know the Old Testament better?

Hopefully you will discover the glory of the old covenant. But remember, it should always point us to the greater glory of the new covenant that is ours in Jesus Christ.

⊡ **explore more**

optional

> **Read Exodus 34 v 29-35**

In Exodus 33, Moses was shown something of God's glory (33 v 12-23), so that when he came back down the mountain, his face was radiant (34 v 29). *Why were the Israelites afraid to come near Moses (v 29-32)?*

Why did they respond with fear, rather than praise and awe? See chapter 32.

Why did Moses wear a veil (34 v 33-35)?

⊡ **investigate**

> **Read 2 Corinthians 3 v 12-18**

5. What makes us bold (v 12)? Compare 1 v 9b-10.

• Look at verses 13 and 18. In what way are Christians bold?

6. Whose minds remain dull, and why (v 13-14)?

7. Who takes the veil away, and when (v 15-16)?

8. What happens when the veil is taken away (v 17-18)?

→ **apply**

9. How does this passage help us to approach God?

10. How does this passage reassure us when we meet people who don't know Jesus?

11. How does this passage challenge us when we meet people who don't know Jesus?

12. What has this session taught you about the privileges Christians have under the new covenant?

⊡ **getting personal**

The greater glory of the new covenant is that Jesus Christ has revealed God to be a God of grace as well as holiness. How much is your relationship with God one of confidence and joy because of his grace? Can you now love and long for his holiness, or does the thought of that still fill you with fear and guilt?

↥ **pray**

Give thanks to God...

- for the new way to himself that he has opened up in Jesus Christ.

- for how he has taken away the veil from your heart so that you can see him in all his glory and grace.

Ask him...

- to help you as you seek to learn from his word more deeply, particularly the Old Testament.

- to open the eyes of those whose hearts are still veiled and who do not know Jesus.

5 FRAGILE YET ETERNAL

2 Corinthians 4 v 1-18

How to keep going

The story so far

True disciples of Jesus Christ will see suffering as part of God's plan to help us grow more like Christ, will be willing to hear and receive God's word, and will love and accept the messenger.

True disciples speak out for Christ even in the face of difficulties or rejection, and have confidence in what Christ has done.

⊕ talkabout

1. What makes it difficult to keep going as a Christian?

• What effect can this have on us?

⬇ investigate

▶ Read 2 Corinthians 4 v 1-18

Because Paul has suffered, some Corinthians don't think he is much of an apostle. In this passage, he explains how he preaches the gospel and keeps going in the face of suffering and opposition.

2. How does Paul preach the gospel (v 1-2, 4-6)?

3. Why don't some understand (v 3-4, and see also 3 v 7-18)?

⊡ apply

4. How might we use deception and distortion of God's word when we share the gospel?

- What is needed for us to share the gospel as Paul shared it?

⊡ getting personal

Who do you need to pray for, asking God to remove the veil that covers their heart? If no one comes to mind, think about how you could find someone to pray for and talk to about Christ.

⬇ investigate

5. What is the treasure that Paul has (v 5-7)?

6. How does having this treasure transform Paul's experience of life (v 8-12)?

7. What does "treasure in jars of clay" tell us about...
- Christian servants of the gospel?

- God's strategy to bring eternal life to people?

8. Why is Paul able to keep on speaking about the gospel (v 13-15)?

• What does this tell us about those who give up speaking about the Christian faith when things get tough?

optional

⊡ **explore more**

In verse 13, Paul quotes Psalm 116.

▶ **Read Psalm 116**

How does this psalm help us to understand how Paul doesn't lose heart?

9. Look at v 16-18 and find more reasons why Paul doesn't lose heart.

➔ **apply**

10. Make a list of all the things Paul has mentioned in this Bible passage that can help us not to lose heart in the face of suffering.

When you are tempted to lose heart, what will keep you going?

As a Christian, what should you look back to? What do you look forward to? What can you trust God to be doing right now?

⬆ **pray**

Give thanks to God...

• for living in us in Jesus Christ.

• for revealing the truth to us, and unveiling our eyes.

Ask Him...

• for courage and perseverance as we seek to live as Jesus' followers.

• for help in sharing the good news of Jesus Christ with others.

2 Corinthians 5 v 1-10

CLOTHED OR NAKED?
Looking ahead to eternity

True disciples of Jesus Christ will see suffering as part of God's plan to help us grow more like Christ, will be willing to hear and receive God's word, and will love and accept the messenger.

True disciples speak out for Christ even in the face of difficulties or rejection, and have confidence in what Christ has done.

True disciples don't lose heart when they face hardship and suffering. They know God is at work in them and will bring them to eternal life.

⊕ **talkabout**

1. What do you think eternal life will be like?

- Are you looking forward to it? Why / why not?

⬇ investigate

▶ Read 2 Corinthians 5 v 1-10

We've seen how Paul keeps his eyes fixed on the resurrection and glory to come, and so doesn't lose heart. Here he goes further, saying more about how we should view the life we have now, compared with the life to come.

DICTIONARY

Judgment seat (v 10): we will all stand before the judgment seat when Jesus returns to judge the world.

2. List the terms Paul uses for "earthly" and "heavenly" dwellings in v 1-5.

• According to Paul, which is the better dwelling?

3. Why do we groan in this body (v 2-4)?

⊡ explore more

optional

In verse 4 of chapter 5, Paul makes an allusion to Isaiah 25 v 8 when he says: "so that what is mortal may be swallowed up by life".

▶ Read Isaiah 25 v 1-12

What does the prophet praise God for in v 1-5?

What does the prophet look forward to in v 6-9?

How does this compare with what Paul waits for?

As well as promising salvation, what else is promised in v 10-12?

4. Why is Paul so confident that "what is mortal [will] be swallowed up by life" (v 4-5)?

5. Where would Paul rather be (v 6-8)? Why?

⮕ apply

6. Christians can look forward to going home to be with the Lord. We can be confident of eternal life. How should this make our lives look different from those around us?

⊡ getting personal

If someone were to follow you closely for a day, would they see that you are looking forward to being at home with the Lord in eternal life? What would give away your true position?

⊡ investigate

7. What should be our response to knowing that Christ will judge all of us (v 9-10)?

8. As followers of Jesus Christ, what will happen to us when we die?

⊟ apply

9. How does our attitude to eternity sometimes differ from Paul's? Why?

- What have we learned this session that will help us keep a right view of our eternal future?

10. How can we go wrong in our attitude to God's judgment?
Why does this happen?

• What have we learned this session that will help us to keep a right view of God's judgment?

getting personal

On a scale of one (not at all) to ten (perfectly), what score would you give yourself for...

• longing for your eternal home with the Lord?

• confidence in God's promise of a new resurrection body?

• perseverance through the groaning of this earthly life?

• seeking to please the Lord in the light of his coming judgment?

pray

Give thanks to God that Christ is coming back, both as Judge and Saviour, and that he will save his people. Thank him that we have the Holy Spirit as a guarantee of what is to come.

Pray for obedience as we await the judgment of God, and give thanks that Christ has taken the punishment we deserve.

7 2 Corinthians 5 v 11-21
LIFE AND DEATH
Why we share the gospel

The story so far

True disciples of Jesus Christ will see suffering as part of God's plan to help us grow more like Christ; will be willing to hear and receive God's word, without contempt for the messenger; will speak out for Christ even in the face of difficulties or rejection; and will have confidence in what Christ has done.

True disciples don't lose heart when they face hardship and suffering. They know God is at work in them and will bring them to eternal life. They live by faith, not by sight—focused on eternity and on pleasing God, and not taken up with life here and now.

⊕ talkabout

1. Think about something that you are known for talking constantly about (eg: football, a musician, a TV programme, etc). Why do you want so much to share that discovery or insight with others?

⊡ investigate

Paul now gives us a masterclass on why and how to share the gospel. He builds on his comments in verses 9-10 about living in the light of what is to come.

▶ Read 2 Corinthians 5 v 11-15

2. Why does Paul share the gospel, even when this causes him suffering (v 11—link this with verses 9-10)?

3. What is his attitude to what others think of him (v 12-13)?

4. Why is Paul compelled by Christ's love (v 14-15)?

→ **apply**

5. Paul was compelled by Christ's love to keep on sharing the gospel, despite persecution and suffering. How do our reasons for sharing the good news with others compare?

    • Why are our attitude and motivation sometimes so different from Paul's?

⊕ talkabout

6. If someone asked you to explain the gospel to them, what would you want to say?

⊕ investigate

> ❯ **Read 2 Corinthians 5 v 16-21**

7. Read through this section again. How does Paul describe what Christ has done for us?

DICTIONARY

Sins/sin (v 19, 21): doing what *we* want instead of what *God* wants. Sin is an attitude of the heart—rebellion against God.

8. Why does Paul regard Christ differently now (v 16-17)?

9. What has God made all those who are reconciled to God (v 18-20)?

10. Look at Paul's explanation of the good news he proclaimed in v 10-21. Complete the table and then summarise the message.

Christ	Us
(v 10)	(v 10)
(v 14)	(v 15)
(v 15)	(v 17)
(v 21)	(v 18)
	(v 19)
	(v 21)
Summary:	

- How does this summary compare with your answer to question 6?

→ apply

11. How should our lives be affected by the truth that…

a. we have a message of reconciliation?

b. we are ambassadors of Christ?

c. we have good news to proclaim?

⊡ getting personal

How are you doing as a minister of reconciliation and an ambassador for Christ? Make a note of what you want to say in future when you share the gospel. Then write down one or more people that you want to share the gospel with.

⬆ pray

Give thanks to God...

• that Jesus Christ died on the cross for our sins.

• that we are a new creation in him and will become the righteousness of God.

• that God chooses to work through us for the salvation of others, making us ministers of his gospel.

Ask God...

• for wisdom and courage as we seek to share the good news with others.

• to help those we wish to share the gospel with.

8 2 Corinthians 6 v 1 – 7 v 1

GRACE, NOT STUMBLING
BLOCKS Helping and being helped

The story so far

True disciples of Jesus will see suffering as part of God's plan to help us grow
more like Christ; will be willing to hear and receive God's word, without
contempt for the messenger; will speak out for Christ even in the face of
difficulties or rejection; and will have confidence in what Christ has done.

True disciples don't lose heart when they face hardship and suffering. They
know God is at work and will bring us to eternal life. They live by faith, not by
sight—focused on eternity and pleasing God, and not on life here and now.

Christ's love compels us to share the gospel of Jesus Christ—so this is what
true disciples will want to do.

⊕ talkabout

1. How close should Christians get in their various relationships with
   unbelievers?

⊕ investigate

> ▶ Read 2 Corinthians 6 v 1-13

DICTIONARY

The day of salvation (v 2): the
time between Jesus' first coming and
his return is the "day" of salvation,
when we may be reconciled to God
through Christ (5 v 20).

2. What do the Corinthians need to do (v 1-2)?
When and why?

3. In verses 4-10 Paul decides to commend himself to the Corinthians as a servant of God. How will this help the Corinthians to receive God's grace?

4. How does Paul commend himself to the Corinthians (v 3-10)?

5. What does Paul want the Corinthians to do (v 11-13)?

6. What will this mean for the Corinthians, in the light of verse 1?

→ **apply**

In this section of the letter in particular, we see how the Corinthians have not been willing to listen to Paul.

7. How can we follow Paul's example and not put stumbling blocks in the way of people hearing God's message?

8. How can we avoid being like the Corinthians who won't listen to Paul?

⊡ **getting personal**

Think about which of these stumbling blocks to hearing the gospel could be lurking in your life: lack of perseverance, little commitment, laziness, impurity, unkindness and impatience, hypocrisy, self-reliance rather than relying on God, or little joy in Christ. Who might be rejecting the gospel because of failings like these in your life? Make it your priority this week to seek God's power and grace to remove these stumbling blocks.

⬇ investigate

❯ Read 2 Corinthians 6 v 14 – 7 v 1

9. What reasons does Paul give for not being "yoked" to an unbeliever (v 14-18)?

10. What, then, does it mean to be yoked to an unbeliever?

⊡ explore more

optional

In 2 Corinthians 6 v 16 and 17, Paul quotes first from Leviticus 26 v 12, and then Isaiah 52 v 11.

❯ Read Leviticus 26 v 1-13

Why do you think Paul quotes from this passage here? What are the parallels between Israel then and Christians now?

❯ Read Isaiah 52 v 1-12

What is happening in this passage (compare Isaiah 48 v 20), and how does it help Paul to make his point?

11. Look at what Paul says in 7 v 1. How does this relate to what he has said in 6 v 1?

➔ apply

12. How are we in danger of being yoked with unbelievers?
What are we going to do about it?

⊡ getting personal

How willing are you right now to hear the challenges as well as the comforts of the gospel? Is there some issue that you are not facing up to? Is there a Christian leader you find it difficult to submit to? Are you resisting the advice of more mature Christians? Don't receive God's grace in vain.

⬆ pray

Give thanks to God for his grace, and the way in which others have shown us what God's word says.

Ask him for...

• perseverance in speaking to others, inside and outside the church, about God and his will for our lives.

• receptive ears and hearts to hear the things we need to hear.

• wisdom as we seek not to be yoked with those who don't know Jesus as Lord and Saviour.

9 2 Corinthians 7 v 2-16
DISCIPLINE AND ENCOURAGEMENT
Responding to godly correction

The story so far

True disciples of Jesus will see suffering as part of God's plan to help us grow more like Christ; will be willing to hear and receive God's word, without contempt for the messenger; will speak out for Christ even in the face of difficulties or rejection; and will have confidence in what Christ has done.

True disciples don't lose heart when they face hardship and suffering. They know God is at work and will bring them to eternal life. They live by faith, not by sight—focused on eternity and pleasing God, and not on life here and now.

Christ's love compels us to share the gospel of Jesus. True disciples of Christ will receive God's grace by repenting when they are challenged by God's word.

⊕ talkabout

1. Have you ever been corrected by a church leader or fellow Christian? How did you respond?

⊕ investigate

In chapter 7, as Paul draws this section of the letter to a close, he returns to some of the issues he has addressed back in chapters 1 and 2—his reasons for writing the Corinthians a painful letter. Paul wants them to continue responding well to correction.

❯ Read 2 Corinthians 7 v 2-16

2. Why does Paul want the Corinthians to make room in their hearts for him (v 2-4)?

Repentance (v 9): turning away from sin and towards God; living for him instead of ourselves.

3. Who comforts Paul, and who comforts Titus here (v 5-7)?

➔ apply

4. Think about the depth of Paul's feelings for the Corinthian Christians. How do your relationships with fellow believers in your church compare?

• What can you do to become more like Paul?

the good book guide to 2 corinthians**49**

⊙ **investigate**

5. Look at the news that Paul receives (v 8-9). What is it that makes him rejoice?

6. What is the difference between godly and worldly sorrow (v 10-11)?

⊡ **explore more**

 Read Revelation 18 v 9-19

In Revelation 18, we read of the fall of the great city, Babylon, and how people mourn for her.

What does worldly grief look like?

7. Who has benefitted from the sending of the letter mentioned here (v 12-16)? And how have they benefitted?

8. Paul talks of his pride in the Corinthians (v 4) and his boasting about them (v 14). What does he boast in?

9. Paul has had to say some hard things to the Corinthians. Apart from being an apostle, what gave him the right to say these things?

→ **apply**

10. From what we have read here, what is the right response to legitimate correction?

11. How can we be ready to accept legitimate correction?

↑ **pray**

Give thanks that God corrects us through his word and through godly Christians, like Paul, in order to grow us as his true disciples.

Ask God...

• for the willingness to accept correction.

• for a love for Christian brothers and sisters that longs to see them grow in true discipleship too.

• for the wisdom to know when to offer correction to others.

true
discipleship

2 Corinthians 1 – 7

LEADER'S GUIDE

Leader's Guide

INTRODUCTION

Leading a Bible study can be a bit like herding cats—everyone has a different idea of what the passage could be about, and a different line of enquiry that they want to pursue. But a good group leader is more than someone who just referees this kind of discussion. You will want to:

- correctly understand and handle the Bible passage. But also…

- encourage and train the people in your group to do this for themselves. Don't fall into the trap of spoon-feeding people by simply passing on the information in the Leader's Guide. Then…

- make sure that no Bible study is finished without everyone knowing how the passage is relevant for them. What changes do you all need to make in the light of the things you have been learning? And finally…

- encourage the group to turn all that has been learned and discussed into prayer.

Your Bible-study group is unique, and you are likely to know better than anyone the capabilities, backgrounds and circumstances of the people you are leading. That's why we've designed these guides with a number of optional features. If they're a quiet bunch, you might want to spend longer on talkabout. If your time is limited, you can choose to skip explore more, or get people to look at these questions at home. Can't get enough of Bible study? Well, some studies have optional extra homework projects. As leader, you can adapt and select the material to the needs of your particular group.

So what's in the Leader's Guide?
The main thing that this Leader's Guide will help you to do is to understand the major teaching points in the passage you are studying, and how to apply them. As well as guidance on the questions, the Leader's Guide for each session contains the following important sections:

THE BIG IDEA

One key sentence will give you the main point of the session. This is what you should be aiming to have fixed in people's minds as they leave the Bible study.
And it's the point you need to head back towards when the discussion goes off at a tangent.

SUMMARY

An overview of the passage, including plenty of useful historical background information.

OPTIONAL EXTRA

Usually this is an introductory activity that ties in with the main theme of the Bible study, and is designed to "break the ice" at the beginning of a session. Or it may be a "homework project" that people can tackle during the week.

So let's take a look at the various different features of a Good Book Guide:

⊕ talkabout

Each session kicks off with a discussion question, based on the group's opinions or experiences. It's designed to get people talking and thinking in a general way about the main subject of the Bible study.

⊕ investigate

The first thing you and your group need to know is what the Bible passage is about, which is the purpose of these questions. But watch out—people may come up with answers based on their experiences or teaching they have heard in the past, without referring to the passage at all. It's amazing how often we can get through a Bible study without actually looking at the Bible! If you're stuck for an answer, the Leader's Guide contains guidance on questions. These are the answers to direct your group to. This information isn't meant to be read out to people—ideally, you want them to discover these answers from the Bible for themselves. Sometimes there are optional follow-up questions (see ⊗ in guidance on questions) to help you help your group get to the answer.

⊡ explore more

These questions generally point people to other relevant parts of the Bible. They are useful for helping your group to see how the passage fits into the "big picture" of the whole Bible. These sections are OPTIONAL—only use them if you have time. Remember that it's better to finish in good time having really grasped one big thing from the passage, than to try and cram everything in.

⊡ apply

We want to encourage you to spend more time working at application—too often, it is simply tacked on at the end. In the Good Book Guides, apply sections are mixed in with the investigate sections of the study. We hope that people will realise that application is not just an optional extra, but rather, the whole purpose of studying the

Bible. We do Bible study so that our lives can be changed by what we hear from God's word. If you skip the application, the Bible study hasn't achieved its purpose.

These questions draw out practical lessons that we can all learn from the Bible passage. You can review what has been learned so far, and think about practical differences that this should make in our churches and our lives. The group gets the opportunity to talk about what they personally have learned.

⊡ getting personal

These can be done at home, but it is well worth allowing a few moments of quiet reflection during the study for each person to think and pray about specific changes they need to make in their own lives. Why not have a time for reporting back at the beginning of the following session, so that everyone can be encouraged and challenged by one another to make application a priority?

⊡ pray

In Acts 4 v 25-30 the first Christians quoted Psalm 2 as they prayed in response to the persecution of the apostles by the Jewish religious leaders. Today however, it's not as common for Christians to base prayers on the truths of God's word as it once was. As a result, our prayers tend to be weak, superficial and self-centred rather than bold, visionary and God-centred.

The prayer section is based on what has been learned from the Bible passage. How different our prayer times would be if we were genuinely responding to what God has said to us through his word.

1
2 Corinthians 1 v 1-11
SUFFERING AND COMFORT
God's work in our troubles

THE BIG IDEA

True disciples of Jesus Christ will see suffering as part of God's plan to help us grow more like Christ.

SUMMARY

Paul has experienced many sufferings because of his faith in Christ—some of them because of his ministry to the Corinthians. However, his sufferings cause him to turn to God for comfort. And so, not only despite his sufferings, but in fact because of them, he is still able to comfort others.

On first reading, 2 Corinthians 1 v 1-11 (or the whole of the first section through to 2 v 4) can appear to be a complex and difficult passage. What we need to recognise here is that Paul is having to defend his ministry to the Corinthians against various attacks and questions, which will become clearer as we work through the letter. In the first chapter there are two problems:

1. Why does an apostle of God suffer (1 v 1-11)?

2. How can an apostle of God make a promise, and then not keep it (1 v 12 – 2 v 4)? We'll look at this second section next time.

OPTIONAL EXTRA

1. Write "God is..." on a piece of paper, and get people to finish off the sentence. You could do this as a starter activity, which will give you an insight into how people in your group view God. Or you could do this as part of the answer to question 3, using the information given in verses 3 and 4.

2. Get people (in pairs or groups if that is helpful) to create a job description for the ideal father. Encourage them to be serious about this. The Bible passage in this session introduces God as "the Father of compassion" (v 3). It would be interesting to find out how similar or different people's views of God are to the job description they have created.

GUIDANCE ON QUESTIONS

1. How do difficulties change people?
The purpose of this opening question is to get people to think about difficult situations, and where they normally go for answers. At this stage, you do not need to define "suffering" too precisely. Help people understand that many different situations could qualify, and that difficulties come in all shapes and sizes. Some answers may highlight how people often change for the worse because of such experiences—they become bitter, mistrustful, anxious, depressed, angry, more selfish etc—reflecting the fact that they have not found the sort of comfort that Paul is confident Christians can find in God. Other answers may identify the fact that suffering can lead to positive changes in people—more empathy and compassion towards fellow sufferers etc. This anticipates Paul's own experiences born out of suffering, seen in this Bible passage.

- **What have you done in the past to cope?** This question prepares the ground for Paul's assertion that God is the sufficient source of comfort we can and should turn to in our troubles.

Suggestions for encouraging discussion:

a. Some people may find it easier to answer generally rather than personally.

b. You could use a flip chart or something similar and get your group to share ideas—helpful for those fearful of saying something wrong. Show that you value all contributions by writing down something each time someone speaks.

c. Alternatively, get people to work in pairs

d. Or to jot down their ideas in the Study Guide.

e. Be prepared to lead the way with honesty, but don't make things up! Your aim is to help people begin the process of reflection.

2. Who comforts who here? God comforts Paul, and Paul comforts others, with the comfort he has received from God. It may be helpful to keep coming back to this, as it is the key to understanding 2 Corinthians 1 v 3-11. You could use this simple diagram:

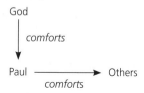

3. How is God described? What does this tell us about his relationship to us and his character? God is described as the God and Father of our Lord Jesus Christ (v 3), the Father of compassion (v 3), and the God of all comfort (v 3). He comforts us in all our troubles (v 4). These verses summarise God's character as our Father—he is compassionate and offers comfort, as a perfect, loving Father.

People may find it helpful here to compare their own experiences of having/being

a father—but be careful, because not everybody's experience of having an earthly father is positive. The emphasis needs to fall on how God is the perfect model of the perfect father—one who truly cares for his children.

4. APPLY: What is the worst trouble that you can imagine striking you? The purpose of this question is to get people to reflect on the all-encompassing phrase "the God of all comfort, who comforts us in all our troubles" (v 3-4), and what that means for their own lives, whatever might happen in the future. There will be a variety of "worst troubles"—being bereaved of husband/wife/children, being rejected by friends or family, losing your sanity, being publicly shamed by failure at work etc. Discuss whatever is relevant to the group.

• **How does the possibility of this kind of trouble affect the way you live now?** Help people to see the connection between these fears and the ways in which they behave eg: fear of losing a child can make parents suffocatingly over-protective; fear of failure can make you constantly cover up or be excessively demanding of people under your supervision; fear of rejection by your family may lead you to keep quiet about your Christian faith and join in with things that you know are wrong etc.

• **How can the phrase "the God of all comfort, who comforts us in all our troubles" transform your life right now?** This question challenges people to get rid of these fears and their destructive influences by trusting in God as their compassionate heavenly Father. Why not get people to memorise this phrase and use it when they talk to each other about difficulties they are going through?

EXPLORE MORE

Make one list of words that describe our Father God, and another list of what he has done. What new insights into God's character have you discovered? If you do this optional section, take the opportunity to reflect on God's character and activity. Here are some of the answers that might be given.

God's character: loving (Ephesians 1 v 4); purposeful (v 5, 9-10, 11); gracious (v 6-7); generous (see "lavished", v 8); sovereign (v 11); merciful (1 Peter 1 v 3); powerful (v 5).

What God has done: He has blessed us with every spiritual blessing in Christ (Ephesians 1 v 3); he chose, predestined and adopted us (v 4-5); he redeemed us through Jesus' blood (v 7); he forgave our sins (v 7); he gave us wisdom and understanding (v 8); he revealed his will to us (v 9); he included us in Christ (v 13); he gave us the Holy Spirit as a deposit of our inheritance (v 14); he has given us new birth (1 Peter 1 v 3); he has given us the hope of resurrection (v 3); he is keeping our inheritance safe (v 4); he is keeping us safe (v 5).

5. What did Christ suffer? You cannot answer this question directly from this passage in 2 Corinthians. It relies, as did Paul, upon the readers having a basic understanding of what Christ did on the cross. As we read the Gospels, we recognise the suffering involved for Jesus in going to the cross—his arrest, punishment and crucifixion. The purpose of this question is to focus the group on what Christ has done, as a necessary preliminary to understanding the next question. It may be helpful for your group to check out some or all of the following verses: Matthew 16 v 21; Hebrews 2 v 9, 18; 5 v 8; 13 v 12; 1 Peter 2 v 23-24.

6. Why does Paul suffer? This question covers both the reason why Paul suffered and the purpose for which he suffered.

v 5: Paul suffers because Christ suffered. As a follower of Christ, he expected to suffer as his Lord suffered, just as a servant follows his master. Jesus himself said this: see Matthew 10 v 22, 24-25.

v 6: Paul suffers for the sake of the Corinthians. First, though not mentioned here, he suffers because of his ministry to the Corinthians—it was Paul's Gentile ministry (his ministry to non-Jews) that eventually got him arrested and sent to Rome in chains. But secondly, seen in v 6, he also suffers as an example to the Corinthians, to help them be patient in sufferings.

Note: Paul's sufferings, as the apostle to the Gentiles, were unique, but the general principle applies to us as it did to him; we can expect to suffer for being a faithful servant of Jesus Christ, whether that means being passed over for promotion, ridiculed, or arrested.

7. How is Paul comforted? Paul receives comfort "from God" (v 4) and "through Christ" (v 5). You may wish to remind people of what was discussed in Explore More above. Or get them to think about what makes following Christ worthwhile, even when it causes us troubles. Answers might include: the comfort of knowing Jesus as Saviour and Lord, of being free from the penalty of sin, or of having a living relationship with Jesus Christ.

8. What do Paul and the Corinthians share? The Corinthians share in Paul's sufferings as they too suffer for the sake of Jesus Christ—they suffer because they live as faithful followers of Jesus. But, at the same time, as true disciples of Christ, they also share in the comfort which Paul receives.

9. APPLY: What troubles have you experienced as a result of being a follower of Jesus Christ? How have you drawn comfort from knowing Jesus as Saviour and Lord? Get people to share difficulties they have experienced as a result of being a follower of Christ. And the comfort people have received from knowing Jesus as their Saviour and Lord. Be willing to share from your own experience.

10. What was the purpose of Paul's sufferings in Asia? Paul suffered in Asia so that he would learn to rely on God (v 9) and place his hope in him for the future (v 10). As Paul faced death, he turned to God. Some members of your group may be concerned that this implies that God caused Paul to suffer in Asia. While the Bible is clear that God is perfectly in control of all situations, in which he is working out his good purposes, notice that Paul's focus here is on God's deliverance (v 10) and faithfulness.

11. What should suffering make us do? You may wish to go back to verses 3 to 6 here. Suffering should make us turn to God for comfort (v 3-5) and rely on him (v 9-10). Then we are enabled to help others (v 5, 6).

⊗

• **What will be lost if we try to rely on ourselves?** This is an important principle: we help others as we rely on God and trust in him. We don't help others by becoming more self-reliant ourselves. We are not to lead people to self-sufficiency, but to God-dependency.

12. APPLY: What will help you to turn to "the God of all comfort" in difficult circumstances? The key here is to stick to specifics. Be ready to give an example from your own life of how you seek to turn to God. If a new group are reluctant to share, try working in pairs. Some ideas for discussion:

• Our own view of God is affected by how much we listen to Bible truth about him, and conversely, by how much we listen to other views about God. How can we make sure we hear truth about God?

• Our readiness to turn to God for comfort will be increased when we remember his faithfulness and compassion in the past (eg: as in question 9 above). When and where can we share stories of God's goodness to us and hear about the experiences of others?

• Which Bible passages encourage us to trust God? How can we keep these in the forefront of our minds?

PRAY
Don't neglect this—and don't forget this too needs careful planning! You may want to encourage people to pray in pairs, if appropriate for your group. It is natural that, given the subject matter of comfort, people will want to pray for others to be comforted. This is fine, but make sure you have enough time to pray along the lines suggested in the Study Guide.

2

2 Corinthians 1 v 12 – 2 v 4

FAITHFUL OR FICKLE?
When plans have to change

THE BIG IDEA

True disciples of Christ will be willing to hear and receive God's word, and will love and accept the messenger.

SUMMARY

This passage follows on from last session. As can be seen later in Paul's letter, particularly from chapter 10 onwards, Paul has been having some problems in Corinth with people who seem more impressive in person than he does. In addition, he has had to say some hard things to the Corinthian church; he mentions a hard letter in 2 v 3 and a "painful visit" in 2 v 1. At the heart of the conflict seems to be the question of Paul's apostleship, and much of the early part of 2 Corinthians is taken up with Paul defending his position as an apostle, and trying to get the Corinthians to understand what true ministry looks like.

Here in the second half of chapter 1 and into chapter 2, Paul is explaining his conduct. In particular, he is explaining why his travel plans have had to change, and why he didn't want to come and see them. Paul begins by talking about boasting, about how the Corinthians need to hear his message (v 12-14), and how his travel plans have had to change (v 15-17). Then he reminds us of the faithfulness of God (v 18-22), before explaining why he did not visit them as initially planned (1 v 23 – 2 v 4). Although his travel plans have had to change, God is unchanging and reliable.

What do we make of all this? The key issue here is the question of boasting in 1 v 12-14. Are the Corinthians willing to boast

in Paul—that is, are they willing to recognise that his holiness, sincerity and grace speak of a man sent by God? Are they also willing to recognise that he is sent from God to them—to God's people? (ie: Are they willing to listen to him?) And for us, are we willing to listen to those God has appointed over us to teach us? Are we willing to listen to God's word? Or will we use the messenger's failings as a reason not to listen?

OPTIONAL EXTRA

(Designed to extend Talkabout) Provide a selection of weekly magazines appropriate for your group—women's, men's, teens', music, sport, property or whatever. Either select some images of people from ads and articles yourself before the session, or give your group a few moments to choose those that attract their eye. Discuss what it is about these images that make these people appear attractive, knowledgeable, trustworthy—in other words, apparently worth listening to and following.

GUIDANCE ON QUESTIONS

1. What kind of people do you find it easiest to listen to? Try to get as many different kinds of answers to this question as possible. For example, answers could include professions (doctor, teacher, perhaps even minister) or characteristics (kind, generous, honest, old and wise). Others may recognise that we listen to people who are like us, or who impress us. Some may even be honest enough to recognise the ways in which perceptions of social class, education, dress and even accent will affect our choice of who we listen to most readily.

- **How do you think the world around us influences our choice of who we listen to most?** Focus on how much image plays a part in how people are presented (this even applies to some of the "Christian" press). This question builds on the previous one—aim for honesty about the kind of things that influence us. See Optional Extra above.

You might want to make a note of what people say here in preparation for application question 10.

2. Why might the Corinthians be reluctant to boast about Paul? (Note: "boast" here has a positive meaning. It means to be openly proud of something or someone that is praiseworthy. If the Corinthians are to boast about Paul, it means that they will recognise that he is sent to them from God and they will be willing to accept what he says.) The Corinthians might be reluctant to boast about Paul because he has had to tell them things which they have only partly understood (v 14). They are not obscure things (v 13) so this suggests they have not wanted to listen. There is also a suggestion in verse 12 that the Corinthians might prefer to listen to "worldly wisdom".

(See also 1 Corinthians 2 v 4-5, part of an earlier passionate plea from Paul to these same Corinthians to disregard the worldly "wisdom" they are so enamoured of and instead accept God's "foolishness".)

⊻

- **What have we already learned about Paul in 1 v 1-11, which may also make the Corinthians reluctant to boast about him?** The Corinthians' reluctance to boast about Paul may result from the fact that he suffers—something which they don't think goes with being an apostle.

3. When will they boast about Paul? The Corinthians will boast about Paul when Christ returns ("the day of the Lord Jesus"—v 14), and the truth is revealed. Paul is confident that they will ultimately recognise the truth about his authenticity as a God-appointed apostle of Jesus Christ.

4. How might the Corinthians view Paul's change of travel plans? They would probably be suspicious of Paul's change of plans, seeing it as a further sign of weakness and vacillation. Not only does he suffer—he also doesn't keep his promises.

5. Paul calls God himself as a witness to his plans. Why is it such a big deal for Paul to show that his change of plans was not because of worldly fickleness? Paul draws a connection between his reliability and his faithful preaching of the gospel (v 19)—the message that demonstrates the supreme faithfulness of God (v 20). Paul is God's messenger, speaking God's word, and God is reliable. Paul wants the Corinthians to recognise that a change in his plans does not mean a change in his character, nor in God's character. (**Note:** In the same way, the experience of suffering does not mean that God's character has changed, or that Paul is not fit to be an apostle—see Session 1.)

6. APPLY: How should Christian leaders help people to take the good news about Jesus Christ seriously? And how can they hinder that? Those in leadership roles have a particular responsibility to lead by their conduct—their sincerity, holiness and grace. (If you want to stress this point, look up the list of qualifications for overseers and deacons in 1 Timothy 3, and note how much is said about character there, and how little about "qualifications".)

- **Why is it important for all Christians, leaders or not, to act with holiness, sincerity and grace?** All Christians are witnesses of the gospel, and should live in a way that makes the Christian message attractive. (See Titus 2 v 1-10, especially v 5, 8 and 10.)

EXPLORE MORE
Summarise what God has done for the Corinthians (and Christians today). How do these truths make our lives different from those around us? God has fulfilled all his promises in Jesus Christ (v 20). He has saved us and given his Holy Spirit as a guarantee that we are hhis and will be his on the last day (v 21-22). This is a good question to spend some extra time on. You may wish to look at passages such as Ephesians 1 v 3-14 (see Session 1) or Romans 3 v 21-26 for a fuller description of how we have been saved.

People may have their own ideas about the practical effects of these truths in the lives of Christians. Here are some possible answers:

- Since all God's promises are fulfilled in Jesus Christ, it is supremely worthwhile to live for him. Don't get distracted by other "gospels" that seek to claim your attention.

- Since all God's promises are fulfilled only in Jesus Christ, he must be the only way to God. This is what we need to be telling people, even though this is deeply politically incorrect today.

- Since it is God who makes us stand firm in Christ, we can be confident that he will keep us safe until Jesus returns. Although we all fail and fall into sin, we need never despair of losing our salvation, because it doesn't depend on us.

- Since God has done all these things for us, all the glory should go to him. There is nothing about our salvation that we have contributed, so no reason to feel that we are better than anyone else.

- Since we have the Holy Spirit now as a guarantee of what is to come, we can live joyfully, whatever our circumstances, full of hope and confidence about our future.

At this point you may want to pause to thank God for all his goodness and great mercy to us in sending his Son and his Spirit.

7. Why didn't Paul go to Corinth? Paul didn't go to Corinth to spare the Corinthians a painful visit. He would rather work through persuasion than confrontation. Notice how Paul's care, compassion and suffering for the Corinthians shine through here.

8. Why was Paul's visit going to be painful? The visit was going to be painful because Paul had already said some hard things (v 4), and still had more hard things to say (v 1-2). And this to people he loved and cared for, who he wanted to rejoice over (v 3).

9. What does this section of the letter tell us about Paul? It is always wise to build a character profile on what we know, rather than on what we don't; and what we know from Paul's letters is that he was warm-hearted and compassionate. Take the opportunity here to emphasise Paul's love and care for the Corinthians, and how painful it was for him to have to correct them. Some Christians have been wrongly taught that Paul was a cold-hearted intellectual, or a misogynist, or "merely an academic" or a social misfit. If you want to tease out this issue, then you may wish to ask this optional extra question:

• What do you think of Paul the apostle? Would you like him to come and stay at your house?

EXPLORE MORE
• **What did Paul do in Corinth? How might the day job have affected some people's view of Paul?** Paul taught and made tents. The tent-making appears to have been another reason why some of the Corinthians looked down on Paul. They seemed to want teachers who were impressive, not those who made tents for a living.

• **Paul's ministry was "successful" in Corinth, but it wasn't easy. How did God reassure him?** With an assurance of his own presence, and of how he was already at work in Corinth: he already had people there (some of whom, quite possibly, were not yet saved.)

• **What do verses 12-17 show us about the relationship between the Jews, Christians and Romans?** It was complicated! Sometimes the Romans protected the Christians; sometimes they persecuted them. Their main concern at this stage, whatever happened later, was for public order. As for the Jews, some persecuted the Christians (as Paul had), but others became Christians themselves.

• **How does this passage help us understand Paul's relationship with the Corinthians?** Notice how Paul, despite considerable hostility, stayed in Corinth for a long time—18 months (v 11). He saw people come to faith there, and he planted the church there. No wonder he cared for them!

10. APPLY: What might we use as a reason not to listen to someone teaching God's word? All the things that were discussed in question 1 could be mentioned here, as well as those things that have come up during the session, including:

• hasty conclusions about people's character (eg: Paul's perceived unreliability).

• lack of mainstream recognition—perhaps no widely recognised qualifications or a reputation as an outsider (eg: Paul was persecuted rather than admired, regarded as a Jew by the Gentiles and too Gentile for the Jews).

• "wrong" social status—not university-educated or white or middle-class (eg: Paul had to work as a tent maker when he first came to Corinth).

• not proclaiming the "right" message (eg: Paul persisted in telling the Corinthians things they clearly didn't want to hear).

Use your notes from earlier to help people. Try not to discuss particular people who might be "difficult" to listen to, but focus on the potential faults in our own perceptions.

Note: Of course, there are people who claim to teach the Bible that we shouldn't listen to. They are those who twist God's word—false teachers. This will often show up in their conduct over time (see Matthew 7 v 15-23).

11. APPLY: How does knowing who God is help us to listen to those who teach his word? However inconsistent and flawed those who teach God's word are, God is consistent and perfect. Therefore his word can be trusted, and anyone who rightly teaches his word should be listened to.

3 2 Corinthians 2 v 5 – 3 v 6
TRUTH AND FORGIVENESS
Speaking out in Christ

THE BIG IDEA
True disciples speak for Christ despite rejection.

SUMMARY
Paul has outlined why he changed his travel plans, and in 1 v 23 – 2 v 4 he has explained that he didn't want to cause the Corinthians grief by another painful visit. Now he turns to two matters. The first concerns the church in Corinth (2 v 5-11): Paul urges the Corinthians to respond to his instruction by showing forgiveness to a repentant sinner. The second is more personal to Paul, but also has a much wider relevance for all believers (2 v 14-17, and into chapter 3): there will always be two responses—negative or positive—to the gospel, but we can be confident about gospel ministry because of Christ.

Both these issues relate to how the Corinthians have responded to Paul in the past, and how they respond now. Clearly, the Corinthians had certain ideas about what was important; as we have seen, some of them struggled to listen to an apostle who suffered! Paul wants them to understand what is truly important.

The first issue here relates to forgiveness. Someone has caused Paul and the Corinthians grief (2 v 5) and has been punished (v 6). But he is repentant, and should be publicly forgiven (v 7-8). Paul had written a painful letter to test them—would they be obedient (v 4, 9)? They were—and passed the test. Now they need to forgive just as Paul has forgiven (v 10), so that there

will be no opportunity for Satan to take advantage of unloving attitudes (v 11). In the light of Paul's leadership here, this session looks at the difficulties we can have in both imposing discipline and demonstrating forgiveness.

Note: Some commentators think that the person mentioned here is the same as the "immoral brother" in 1 Corinthians 5. This is possible, but by no means certain. It would be better therefore to resist this identification, and recognise that we do not know for certain who this was, or what they had done. This does not affect the meaning of this section: the repentant sinner should be forgiven.

Then Paul turns to reflecting on the response to his own ministry. He went to Troas and found gospel opportunities, but no Titus (v 12-13). Anxious for the Corinthians, he went on to Macedonia. At this point in the letter, Paul begins to look at Christian ministry in general, looking at how the good news of Jesus Christ is received (v 14-16), how it should be preached (v 17), and how, because of Christ, we can always be confident in gospel ministry, however unequal to the task we feel (2 v 16b; 3 v 4-6).

What ties these two sections together are the issues of right conduct—here, speaking out as a minister of Christ (even though the message is painful, or provokes rejection), and making a right response to that message.

OPTIONAL EXTRA

This could be a light-hearted starter activity, or used as an extension to questions 6 and 7. It relates to 2 v 15-16, which describes the "aroma of Christ" as "an aroma that brings death" to some people and at the same time "an aroma that brings life" to others. Get a selection of scented products—they shouldn't all be ones that you like, and make sure you include some that will divide opinion. Pass them around and get people to choose the ones that they like and dislike the most. Aim to find out which scents produce the strongest positive and negative reactions. Ask your group what it is that can make Christians "smell" like this to the people around them.

GUIDANCE ON QUESTIONS

1. Think of situations in which you know you should speak out, but find it very difficult to do so. Why do you fail to do the right thing? There are a variety of reasons. It's likely that some of these will be connected to a fear of people's hostility and rejection, or to a lack of competence. Both issues are touched on in this session, where we will see that Paul was unafraid to say difficult things both inside and outside the church. Inside the church, he tested the obedience of the Corinthians to his apostolic authority, by pointing out error and instructing the church to exercise discipline, and then, later, by instructing them to forgive the repentant sinner. Outside the church, Paul continued to spread the gospel of Christ, though it was a task to which he clearly felt unequal, and provoked a sharp division among those who heard the message. In all of this difficult speaking, Paul acted as a man sent by God, and in total reliance on him.

2. Someone has caused grief by his actions. Who did he grieve? Paul and the Corinthians have both been hurt by the person's actions. However, it seems to be mostly Paul—his grief is mentioned first in verse 5, and he sets an example of forgiveness in verse 10. Many commentators believe that the problem here was a challenge to Paul's authority, hence the comment in verse 9.

3. This person has been disciplined. Find two reasons why Paul now calls for forgiveness. The person needs to be forgiven (1) because he has repented (v 6-7), and (2) so that the devil won't get a foothold ("for your sake, in order that Satan might not outwit us", v 10-11). Refusal to forgive this person may lead to a dispute and then dissension among the believers (note, v 6, that it is a majority, not everyone, involved in disciplining this person). The resulting damage to the unity of the church, its reputation and the faith of individual Christians would be all that Satan could wish for. Forgiveness does not mean that the person, if a leader, will necessarily be restored to his previous role. But he will be restored to the fellowship.

EXPLORE MORE

- **What does Jesus say about forgiveness in Luke 17 v 3-4?** Jesus says we should continue to forgive the repentant brother, even if he is a repeat offender. Notice that forgiveness here is based on the existence of true repentance.

- **What do you think the connection is between v 1-2 and 3-4?** The link is the same as that found in 2 Corinthians—giving the devil a foothold = causing "one of these little ones to stumble" (v 2), here by failing to forgive them, and thus provoking resentment etc.

4. APPLY: Why is discipline sometimes so difficult to do—and to accept? It feels unloving because it is painful (see Hebrews 12 v 11a). You could ask the following questions to tease out the issues here.

⊠

- **Why is discipline particularly difficult in western culture?** Because the high value that is placed on individual autonomy leads people to be especially suspicious of authority and any pressure to make people conform to an objective standard or truth.

- **Why is discipline difficult in any culture?** Because our sinful nature craves the freedom to do what we want (see Romans 8 v 5a; Ephesians 2 v 3), and leads us to despise all authority (see 2 Peter 2 v 10), including God's. Even as Christians, we still have to struggle with the sinful nature (see Galatians 5 v 17), so it will not be surprising that we may struggle to accept the idea of discipline in the church.

- **What will help us to impose discipline or support our leaders in doing so?** See Hebrews 12 v 5-11. God's discipline is a proof that he loves us as his children. In the short term discipline is painful, but in the long term it produces a harvest of righteousness and peace. Sharing God's view of discipline will help us act on this issue and respond to it in the right way.

5. APPLY: Why is forgiveness sometimes so difficult? Many reasons could come up here: how bad the wrong was, lack of repentance (note that this section is not dealing with forgiving the unrepentant), continuing effects of the hurt, a desire for revenge etc. These responses are important and need to be explored. However, with the possible exception of a lack of repentance, none of them are a reason not to forgive. (Be aware that for some in your group this may be a very painful "live" issue, and the idea of forgiveness will be very challenging for them. You will need to think about how you can offer personal help to someone like this.)

- **How does the passage help us to be more forgiving?** The passage contains a command to forgive (v 7) and a reason to forgive (v 11). We should seek to remember both. (**Note:** The New Testament is clear about the Christian obligation to forgive others. See Matthew 18 v 21-35.)

Note: Verses 12-13: When Paul went to Troas, he found the door open for the gospel, but he had no peace because he didn't find Titus, and therefore didn't know how his "hard" letter to the Corinthians had been received (see 2 Corinthians 7 v 6-7, 13; 8 v 16, 23).

6. Paul describes himself and other gospel teachers as "the pleasing aroma of Christ". What creates this "smell"? The aroma is the knowledge of Christ, which has been spread among the Corinthians and others by the apostles ie: it is the preaching of the gospel of Jesus Christ.

7. How do different people respond to the fragrance? For the perishing it is the smell of death, as they continue to reject the good news of Jesus Christ. (**Note:** This is not talking about how these people feel about the gospel message, but about the fact that they face eternal condemnation because they have rejected God's only way of salvation—compare John 3 v 36.) For those who are being saved it is the fragrance of life, as God saves them through the preaching of the gospel, and as continued exposure to the good news strengthens them in the faith.

8. How does Paul feel about his role and how does he approach it? He recognises that he is not equal to the task of being the messenger of life and death (v 16). However, he approaches his task in reliance upon God, seen from the way he acts before God (v 17) and what we have already seen in the letter (1 v 9). He can do the job that God wants him to do because he has been sent by God (v 17).

⊻

• **We too are to spread the good news about Jesus Christ. If, like Paul, we are doing this in reliance on God, how will we go about it? And how not?** Those who communicate the good news of Jesus Christ, if they are relying on God to do this, will not be like those who peddle goods—who are in the business of making sales and, by implication, are happy to change what they sell to suit the market. Instead, they will act with sincerity, speaking before God and being concerned with what God wants, not with what people want. Discuss with your group how we are sometimes tempted to change the gospel to make it "sell" better.

9. Why doesn't Paul need letters of recommendation to the Corinthians? Paul doesn't need letters of recommendation to or from the Corinthians because he knows them, and they know him—and his ministry among them has already been written on their hearts. (Note that the contrast between hearts and tablets of stone prepares for the contrast which Paul makes

between his own and Moses' ministry in 3 v 7-18, see Session 4.)

• **What was important to some of the Corinthians?** A person's reputation. They were only willing to accept Paul's authority as an apostle if other Christians commended him to them.

• **What was important to Paul?** Paul was not concerned with what other people thought of him, but with what God thought of him. "We speak before God … as those sent from God" (2 v 17). He measured his ministry not by what other people said about him but by lives changed by the Spirit as a result of hearing the gospel (3 v 3).

Note: It is fear of what others think that makes us weak in speaking out as Christian leaders and ministers of the gospel; but if we have Paul's attitude, we will be bold to speak what is right, regardless of the consequences.

10. Where does Paul's competence come from? From God. Again, note that God has done a new thing in Paul and the other apostles, by making them ministers of the Spirit. (**Note:** Verse 6b = where the law condemned because no one could keep it [see Galatians 3, especially verse 10], the Spirit gives life through the death and resurrection of Jesus Christ.)

11. APPLY: How can Paul's perspective on evangelism help us as we talk to others? Use the following questions, if needed, to help people work out the answer to this question:

⊻

- **What can help us when we feel we lack the competence to tell people the gospel?** Even the apostle Paul, who contributed more to the writing of the New Testament than any other apostle or first-century Christian, did not think that he was competent to tell people the gospel. But that is the very thing that makes us depend on God, who is supremely competent—compare 1 v 8-9.

- **What can help us when we are discouraged by negative reactions to our evangelism?** As we share the good news with others, we can trust in God for the outcome. We need to recognise that some will reject the good news, and this is not necessarily because we have done a bad job of communicating. In fact, this passage indicates that it is precisely when the gospel is communicated effectively (bringing the fragrance of life to some) that it will provoke hostility and be rejected (bringing the smell of death to others). Instead of being discouraged, we seek prayerfully to share the gospel, trusting that God will lead us, and that the Holy Spirit will work in people's lives to bring them to God.

12. Look back at the situations discussed in question 1. How different is Paul in his commitment to speak out as a minister of Christ? Nothing sways Paul from his determination to speak for Christ, whether that involves the unpleasant task of rebuking fellow Christians, insisting on a difficult course of action like forgiveness, or spreading the gospel among those who will reject it.

- **What explains that difference?** This question reviews the things learned from this Bible passage. A number of pointers to Paul's faithfulness can be identified here:

- He deeply loves his Christian brothers and sisters (2 v 1-4, 8).

- He is aware of how the devil can outwit God's people (v 11).

- He is confident that God is at work, whatever happens (v 14-16).

- He views himself as a man "sent from God" (it means he doesn't try to "sell" the gospel to people) (v 17).

- He is not interested in his reputation with other people, but with how God views him (shown by the way the Spirit changes people through his ministry) (3 v 1-3).

- He relies on God, not on himself, to make him a competent minister of the gospel (v 4-6).

Note: While Paul's role as an apostle gave him a unique responsibility and authority, there are many parts of his ministry that church leaders, and ordinary Christians as well, should be involved in today. Church leaders are responsible for disciplining church members and restoring those who repent. All Christians are called to be witnesses of the gospel.

2 Corinthians 3 v 7-18
THE OLD AND THE NEW
The difference that Christ makes

THE BIG IDEA
True disciples of Christ will have confidence in what Christ has done.

SUMMARY
This passage follows on from 3 v 1-6, where Paul began the contrasts which mark this section (see 3 v 3 and 6: ink/Spirit, stone/hearts, death/life). However, the explicit contrast doesn't begin until 3 v 7, so that is a good place to focus this session.

The emphasis falls on the glory of the old covenant or ministry (five times the old covenant is described as glorious in verses 7-11), and how that glory is surpassed by the new. Don't be tempted to lessen the value of the old covenant—it provided genuine, if temporary, access to God, and looked forward (particularly in the Passover) to what Christ would do on the cross. However, the new eclipses the old.

The link between verses 16 and 17 can also seem unclear. The link between freedom and the veil is that when the veil is removed, there is freedom in the Spirit from bondage to the law, which condemns (v 9), and we can be transformed into the likeness of Christ. The overall aim is to show that we can have a confidence in the new covenant, a confidence that will make us bold.

Paul's original readers clearly understood what was meant by the terms "old and new covenant", but there may be people in your group who have very little knowledge of the Bible. You will need to think how you can simply explain to them the old and new covenants, at the start of this session.

OPTIONAL EXTRA
This is a starter activity that will give you some idea of how your group views and understands the Old Testament (see question 1). Draw up a "Test yourself" survey with responses to the Old Testament, and either get your group to fill it in during the session, or give it to people before they come. People should rate statements like the following ones between 0 (don't agree) and 5 (totally agree).

- We don't need to read the Old Testament nowadays.

- The book of Leviticus has nothing to say to me.

- The Old Testament has a different view of God to the New Testament.

- I don't think we need to follow Old Testament laws at all.

- The Old Testament was for the Jews and the New Testament is for Christians.

- The Old Testament is more difficult to understand than the New Testament.

- You can't understand the Old Testament without the New Testament.

- You can't understand the New Testament without the Old Testament.

This is a complex area but this session will help your group to understand both the importance and the limitations of the Old Testament's revelation of God.

GUIDANCE ON QUESTIONS

1. When someone mentions "history", what other words come to mind? Depending on your group, you'll get a mixture of responses here. Some people might give you dates (1066 and so on). Other responses might include: "boring", "old fashioned", "irrelevant", "academic" and so on. You could ask the following optional extra question if you have time for a longer discussion:

• **How important is it for us to understand history today?**

• **How similar are your feelings about the Old Testament?** You might want to provide some descriptive words and phrases to help people identify their view of the Old Testament, or even write them up on a board/flipchart for people to circle those words/phrases they agree with. (See Optional Extra above.)

2. Look at how Paul compares the old and new covenants and complete the table. An example of how the table might be filled in:

Old covenant (ministry that brought death)	New covenant (ministry that brings life)
(v 7) engraved in letters on stone	(v 8) ministry of the Spirit
(v 7, 11) fading glory	(v 11) lasting glory
(v 9) condemns people	(v 9) brings righteousness
(v 10) glorious	(v 10) surpassing glory

3. What does Paul do in these verses to show us just how amazing the new covenant is? He first points out how glorious the old was, and then shows how much more glorious the new is.

4. APPLY: How can we remind ourselves of the glory of the old covenant? The only way is by reading God's word and listening to faithful teaching of God's word—including the Old Testament, of course, but also by looking out for the way in which the New Testament uses and explains the Old.

• **Discuss why people find it difficult to read or learn from the Old Testament. What sort of things can help us overcome this?** This is an opportunity for your group to raise particular difficulties that they have with understanding and learning from the Old Testament. Choose what is most appropriate for your group from the following selection of problems:

a. It may be something as simple as not knowing the Old Testament stories and how they fit together, in which case you may want to suggest an extra session or sessions to introduce people to this. Come prepared with some suggestions for books to buy, or a Bible timeline poster to look at, or a reference book that people could borrow.

b. People may simply find it hard to get motivated to learn from the Old Testament because they believe, now that Jesus has come, that it is completely irrelevant. Already this session has shown that idea to be a fallacy, but it may be helpful to show them God's purpose behind the Old Testament. Use the following questions:

• **What would you say was the purpose of the Old Testament, and the old covenant which it contains?** (See Romans 3 v 19-21 and Galatians 3 v 21-25.) Romans 3: The law (old covenant) could make no one righteous; it could only show people that they were sinners, v 20, and point to the new covenant, a righteousness from God, apart from law, v 21. Galatians 3: The law (old covenant) leads us to Christ, who can justify us, v 24.

• **How do we lose out if we don't know about the Old Testament and the old covenant?** We don't appreciate how hopeless our predicament is without Jesus and the new covenant.

c. People may be wary of the Old Testament because they have come across some weird practice or view adopted by applying the Old Testament directly to our age, in which case you will need to talk about how the Old Testament primarily teaches us about the promises and need for a Saviour that only Jesus Christ fulfils and meets.

• **If we don't understand the purpose of the Old Testament and old covenant, we will learn and teach wrong things from this part of the Bible. Can you think of any examples of this?** A common mistake is to apply the teaching of the Old Testament directly to ourselves, when in fact it should be teaching us about Jesus Christ—it is the teaching about him that we should

apply directly to ourselves. For instance, Christians don't celebrate the Passover, build a tabernacle/ temple, have priests, go to war against pagan nations etc. because all these things are fulfilled by Jesus Christ. The New Testament shows that he is our Passover Lamb (1 Corinthians 5 v 7), our temple (John 2 v 19-22), our high priest (Hebrews 7 v 23-27), and our all-conquering King (1 Corinthians 15 v 20-26).

EXPLORE MORE

• **Why were the Israelites afraid to come near Moses?** Because his face shone, and they knew this was because he had met with God.

• **Why did they respond with fear, rather than praise and awe?** They were afraid because they had sinned (chapter 32), whereas God, through the law given to Moses, had revealed himself as an absolutely holy God.

• **Why did Moses wear a veil?** To protect the Israelites from seeing even God's reflected glory. This is an indication of the glory of the old covenant—it was God's covenant with his people, and therefore glorious. And yet, its effect was to contrast God's holiness with the sin of his people, producing such terror that the Israelites needed the protection of Moses' veil.

5. What makes us bold? Compare 1 v 9b-10. The hope of the new covenant, and all that it is, makes us bold. 1 v 9b-10: The hope that Christ's new covenant gives us is that God will raise us from the dead and deliver us from deadly peril. Ask your group what is the deadly peril that God supremely saves us from through Jesus Christ (the wages of sin, which is eternal death).

- **Look at 3 v 13 and 18. In what ways are Christians bold?** Christians are bold because, unlike Moses, we do not "protect" people from seeing the full glory of God reflected in us. In other words, the lives and words of Christians reveal to the world around us a God who is holy and yet gracious, who judges all sin but who can forgive sinners. Because we are confident through Jesus Christ that God will deliver us from his judgment, we can also be confident in proclaiming the gospel of God's grace to the world. Contrast those who are not confident of being saved from God's judgment—they will lack boldness in proclaiming God's holiness (because it's too uncomfortable) or his grace (because they are not sure of it for themselves). So in their own lives and words, they will be unable to show others the true glory of God.

6. Whose minds remain dull, and why?
The Israelites (those that follow the law) remain dull, unless Christ removes the veil. Paul is not saying that the Jews are worse than those who don't believe anything; he is just explaining why not all of the Jews have come to follow Jesus, the true Messiah.

Note: In verses 12 to 18, the reference to the veil shifts. In verse 13 it is the veil on Moses' face; then, from verse 14 onwards, it is the veil that stops people understanding the glory of the new covenant until Christ takes it away. In verse 13 the veil protects: in verse 14, it hinders. Understanding this really helps in understanding the passage.

7. Who takes the veil away, and when?
Christ takes the veil away, when people turn to him.

What part do people play in removing the veil from their own hearts? Because people are veiled, they will not be able to remove their own veils. Christ must act so that they can turn to the Lord. See how Ephesians 2 v 1-9 talks about turning from our old way of life and becoming a Christian: we were "dead", v 1; God "made us alive", v 4-5; God "raised us up with Christ", v 6; see v 8 especially.

8. What happens when the veil is taken away?
People experience freedom (v 17)—freedom from the death penalty for sin, and therefore freedom from fear—and their transformation into Christ-like people begins (v 18).

- **What will it look like when someone receives the Spirit ie: becomes a Christian?** Once we have the Spirit, our lives should begin to change. Although this transformation will not be completed until heaven, we can expect it to start now. **Pastoral note:** Some may struggle with the reality of ongoing transformation in their own lives. Seek to reassure people that God works patiently with us, but be prepared to challenge those who are comfortable in making no progress.

9. APPLY: How does this passage help us to approach God?
Because of the old covenant (the law), the Israelites knew that God was holy and must punish their sin, so when they saw a glimpse of his majesty—even when it was only reflected in the face of Moses—they were terrified. Whereas,

because of the new covenant (the gospel), we know that our holy God has punished our sin in Jesus Christ, and so he shows grace to anyone who is in Christ. This means we can understand more and more of God's majesty and yet still have confidence to approach him. The revelation that God is a God of grace, as well as a God of holiness, is the greater glory of the new covenant.

• **What difference should this make to our daily lives?** We should be willing and eager to pray to God—confessing our sins, thanking him for the gospel of grace, and confiding our problems and fears in him.

10. APPLY: How does this passage reassure us when we meet people who don't know Jesus? We can be confident that Christ will work to remove the veil covering people's hearts when and as he wishes to. Our responsibility is to preach the gospel: it is Christ who works salvation in their hearts.

11. APPLY: How does this passage challenge us when we meet people who don't know Jesus? We should want their veil to be removed—we should pray for it, and share the good news with them.

12. APPLY: What has this session taught you about the privileges Christians have under the new covenant? This is

an opportunity for people in your group to share what has struck them most profoundly in this session. From this passage we have learned a number of things that Christians can do and enjoy because of what Jesus Christ did on the cross, which were not available to God's Old Testament people:

• Christians have the privilege of knowing and displaying to the world a God who is both majestically holy and yet also gracious to sinners.

• We can be bold in declaring God's gospel of grace to sinners because of our confident hope in Christ that God will deliver us from his own judgment on sin.

• We can see God's majesty and yet be free from fear (terror) of him.

• As sinners saved by grace, we reflect God's glory to the world, and increasingly so as we become more like Christ.

• As we show God's glory to the world through the gospel, Christ is at work in people's hearts to save them.

You could also ask your group to think of other things not mentioned in this passage eg: we can call God "Father"—a closer relationship than even Moses had with God. This question is a good way to begin the prayer time, by thanking God for all that he has done in Jesus Christ. You may wish to reflect on what you have learned about this in the four sessions so far.

5

2 Corinthians 4 v 1-18

FRAGILE YET ETERNAL
How to keep going

THE BIG IDEA

True disciples of Christ don't lose heart when they face hardship and suffering. They know what God has done in Christ. They know he is at work in them and will bring them to eternal life.

SUMMARY

In this section of 2 Corinthians, Paul continues to defend himself and his ministry against some of the suggestions of the Corinthians, and to explain to them how a ministry marked by suffering and hardships can be the genuine article. So, in 4 v 1-6 we read again of the gospel that Paul proclaims and how he proclaims it, before he reflects on the treasure we have been given in the gospel in 4 v 7-18.

In this second section, we see that, as followers of Christ, we have treasure in jars of clay—highlighting God's power in contrast to our weakness (4 v 7-12). We believe—and therefore we speak, despite the suffering that can result (see Psalm 116 v 10). We can keep speaking out the gospel because we trust in the God who has power over death (4 v 13-15). We don't lose heart (4 v 16—see 4 v 1) because we live in the light of eternity.

OPTIONAL EXTRA

Divide your group into pairs or small teams. Give each team a photocopy of a line-drawing (perhaps from a child's activity book) and a selection of coloured pencils, felt-tip pens or crayons. Select one item, shape or symbol in the drawing (not the main focus of the picture if possible) and ask each team

to make that item stand out as much as possible as they colour the picture, which they can do in any way they wish—it doesn't have to be realistic. The successful teams will opt for a strong contrast between the item and the rest of the picture eg: dark versus light, cool versus hot colours, faint pencil versus bold felt-tip pen etc. Ask your group to think of other situations in which a strong contrast is used to focus attention on something eg: a brilliantly sparkling jewel displayed on a dark matt background; a spotlight on a darkened stage; a soloist hitting a high note over a low orchestral melody; fluorescent-coloured jackets worn by workmen on a building site; the bright red breast of a robin etc. Today's session shows how God's power and glory revealed in the gospel is highlighted in this way because it is at work in weak and suffering Christians— Paul describes it as "treasure in jars of clay".

GUIDANCE ON QUESTIONS

1. What makes it difficult to keep going as a Christian? People could mention many things here. Some will find continuing to believe a struggle, and therefore will be prone to sin and other expressions of unbelief. Others will struggle with sin—with not being able to overcome it, or (seemingly) to make any progress. Some may have difficulties with specific doctrines, while others will experience sufferings or other difficult life-situations (eg: being married to a non-Christian) which make it hard to keep going.

Note: While the particular situation that Paul addresses here is externally caused suffering, the remedy—to recall and live by the truth revealed by Jesus Christ about himself—is applicable to all these situations.

• **What effect can this have on us?** In particular, you could ask your group about the effect of downheartedness on sharing the gospel with others. In this session (see question 2) we will see that Paul clearly connects downheartedness with deception and distortion in proclaiming the gospel (v 1-2).

2. How does Paul preach the gospel? Openly, honestly, fully, plainly and truthfully—he emphasises an open statement of the truth. He is not afraid to proclaim Jesus Christ as the image of God (v 4) and Lord (v 5), even though it is this kind of teaching that can provoke persecution.

⊻

• **Look for the link between verses 1 and 2. Why is it that some people might use deception and distortion of God's word?** Because they have lost heart ie: they have become discouraged by the difficulties of living as Christians —in particular, the offence/persecution that results when people hear the gospel teaching about Jesus Christ. Paul is clear that preaching the gospel openly and clearly is an expression of not losing heart—v 1.

3. Why don't some understand? Because the gospel is veiled. This veil can only be removed by Christ, acting through his Holy Spirit (3 v 14-18). In the meantime, people are blinded to the truth so won't understand and appreciate the gospel. At this point you could recap Session 4, questions 10 and 11 by asking the following question:

⊻

• **What are the implications of this for when we share the good news of Jesus Christ?** We need to remember that the Holy Spirit must work in order for someone to be saved. There is an encouragement and a challenge in this— to share the gospel faithfully, and to trust in the work of the Holy Spirit in people.

4. APPLY: How might we use deception and distortion of God's word when we share the gospel? Get your group to think about parts of the gospel message which provoke hostility and rejection from non-Christians (eg: sin, judgment, hell, Jesus is the only way of salvation, the lordship of Christ). Encourage people to share from their own experiences and observations how these difficult truths are often covered up or downplayed, and how they themselves have been tempted to do this.

• **What is needed for us to share the gospel as Paul shared it?** You could use the following optional extra question to help your group think about how Paul kept going in gospel ministry.

⊻

• **Why was Paul able to continue his gospel ministry without losing heart, even as he suffered for doing it?** See 4 v 1: "God's mercy"—both in the message (1 v 9b -10) and in his ministry (3 v 5-6). See also 4 v 2: "in the sight of God" (cf. 2 v 17).

First we need to get our thinking straight. Only those who understand the depths of God's mercy and the fact that everything we do is in the sight of God will be able to keep going without losing heart in the very thing—faithful, truthful gospel ministry—that causes us difficulties from others. Then we need to evaluate how openly and plainly we are preaching the gospel.

5. What is the treasure that Paul has?
Paul's treasure is the knowledge of the glory of God in Jesus Christ—the knowledge that Jesus is God's Son, that he alone reveals God's glory, and that he is the one who makes a relationship with God possible. This treasure is within Christians—a real relationship with Christ, the indwelling of the Holy Spirit—and we are to share it with others by proclaiming Christ as Lord.

⊻

• **In verse 6 Paul quotes from Genesis 1 v 3. What do this quotation and the mention of God's light tell us?** The Genesis quote tells us that in being made a Christian, God does something in us as powerful as the act of creating the universe—we become a new creation (5 v 17). The mention of light suddenly switched on in darkness graphically conveys the total transformation that takes place when someone becomes a Christian, from being lost, fearful, helpless and invisible to the joy of seeing, knowing and delighting in the glory of God.

6. How does having this treasure transform Paul's experience of life? You could use the following questions to help your group understand Paul's explanation of his experiences in verses 8-12.

⊻

• **What has been Paul's experience as a minister of the gospel?** He has been hard pressed, perplexed, persecuted and struck down (v 8-9).

• **How does this reflect Jesus' experience?** He suffered at the hands of those who rejected his message, and was finally crucified by them.

• **What was the result of Jesus' suffering?** He atoned for sins, and rose to life again, opening up the way for sinners to be forgiven by God and receive eternal life.

• **What is the result of Paul's suffering (v 10-12)?** His suffering for the message of Jesus Christ demonstrates the reality of what Christ himself has done, bringing life to those, like the Corinthians, who receive the gospel.

• **What is not the result of Paul's suffering (v 8-9)?** He is not crushed, despairing, abandoned or destroyed.

Paul has experienced tremendous suffering as a result of following Christ. But he has treasure within—the knowledge and personal experience of Christ's work. So, although he suffers (he carries around in his body the death of Jesus, v 10), he is never defeated. Paul may be experiencing "death"—and yet he knows that he has life in Jesus Christ. But more than that, it's for the sake of the gospel (and therefore of the Corinthians) that Paul is given over to this experience of death. He is willing to carry on despite his sufferings because this is how the eternal life won by Jesus comes to the Corinthians.

7. What does "treasure in jars of clay" tell us about...

• **Christian servants of the gospel?** We are the jars of clay—we are nothing special in ourselves and, in fact, in human terms, we are not suitable for the purpose of displaying God's treasure. One implication of this is that Christians don't need to wait until they have turned into some kind of super saint (or to be articulate, charismatic, a doctor of theology etc) before they are fit to be witnesses of Jesus Christ. God uses ordinary, even weak people—in fact, sinners, but ones saved by his grace—to bring the gospel of Jesus Christ to the world.

• **God's strategy to bring eternal life to people?** His strategy is to use weak and suffering Christians. Then the treasure of the gospel will be seen to be from God, and not merely a human idea or movement. The implication of this is that when Christians suffer persecution for their faith, we should be confident that God is powerfully at work to save people. This goes against an idea in vogue today that Christians need successful names and celebrities to be most effective in evangelism.

• **If appropriate, get your group to share examples of Christians' suffering and persecution that have made them a powerful witness of the gospel.**

8. Why is Paul able to keep on speaking about the gospel? Paul can speak because he believes (v13)—he trusts in the resurrection (v 14) and he knows that sharing the gospel brings people to salvation and glory to God (v 15).

• **What does this tell us about those who give up speaking about the Christian faith when things get tough?** True belief is seen in outward actions. Here, Paul's trust in what Jesus Christ has done, and in what God is doing through this message, is seen in the fact that he speaks out the Christian message, despite

the persecution this can provoke. Those who give up speaking for Christ show that they do not truly believe in the gospel.

EXPLORE MORE
How does Psalm 116 help us to understand how Paul doesn't lose heart? In Psalm 116 an unnamed Israelite is experiencing hardship and trouble (v 3)—and yet he knows God hears and answers his cry for mercy (v 1-2), and he knows that what he has received from God far outweighs any hardship he may experience now (v 12-13). Paul has, and wants others to have, that same trust and confidence in the Lord that will ensure we do not lose heart.

9. Look at v 16-18 and find more reasons why Paul doesn't lose heart. Paul contrasts the outer with the inner, the temporary with the eternal, and the seen with the unseen. And he chooses to live by what is inner, eternal and unseen, rather than by what is outer, temporary and seen. Despite appearances and what he might be experiencing now in terms of suffering, he knows that God is at work in him (v 16) and that the glory to come far outweighs what he experiences now (v 17-18).

10. APPLY: List the things Paul has mentioned that can help us not to lose heart in the face of suffering. The list will include: God's mercy (v 1); the treasure and power of the gospel (v 6-7); God's purposes worked out in our suffering (v 7-12); the fact of Christ's resurrection and the promise of ours (v 13-14); the opportunity to share the good news now and the joy of seeing God's grace reach others (v 15); keeping our eyes fixed on what is to come, unseen for now but eternal (v 16-18). There will be other things mentioned—spend some time working through this with the group.

6

2 Corinthians 5 v 1-10

CLOTHED OR NAKED?
Looking ahead to eternity

THE BIG IDEA
True disciples of Christ live by faith, not by sight—focused on eternity and on pleasing God, not taken up with life here and now.

SUMMARY
Paul is continuing his theme from chapter 4—see "for" or "now" in verse 1. He has been talking about our eternal future, and now he expands that discussion. In 5 v 1-5, Paul draws a contrast between our earthly and heavenly dwellings—between our present groaning and burdens (examples of which he has already described in 4 v 8-12, and in 1 v 8) and what is to come. He wants the Corinthians to have confidence in the heavenly dwelling that God has prepared for us, and so to be looking forward, not to death, but to resurrection.

Paul is confident (v 6)—he would rather be with the Lord. But in the meantime, his view of the future—of judgment as well as resurrection—leads him to focus on pleasing God in the present.

Note: Paul doesn't say anything here about how, in Jesus Christ, we escape from judgment, but he does talk about this in the next section, particularly in 5 v 21. In discussing God's judgment in questions 7 and 8, don't let your group lose sight of Jesus' death on the cross for us, and the fact that the price has been paid. In mentioning judgment in verse 10, Paul wants to guard against complacency, and motivate all his readers to turn to Christ for forgiveness and mercy.

OPTIONAL EXTRA
(Relates to 5 v 1-4, see question 2 below.) Get your group to list the disadvantages of living in a tent and the advantages of living in a house. You could ask someone to "sell" living in a tent to the group for one minute, and get people to raise objections. Or find pictures or an article about living in a refugee camp, and discuss what life might be like in such temporary and insubstantial accommodation. Or share stories of some camping trip disasters.

GUIDANCE ON QUESTIONS
1. What do you think eternal life will be like? Are you looking forward to it?
Depending on people's Christian experience and maturity, answers here will vary. Some may have an "angels on white clouds" view, which owes more to old religious paintings than to the teaching of the Bible—while others may have an understanding more in line with the Bible's promise of a new heaven and a new earth.

Note: This passage does not discuss in detail what eternal life will be like. The purpose of this question is to focus people on the promised new heaven and earth, and on the idea of looking forward to it, so that we are ready to engage with what Paul has to say about now and the future.

2. List the terms Paul uses for "earthly" and "heavenly" dwellings.
Earthly: tent, is being or will be destroyed (v 1); where we groan and are burdened, what is mortal (v 4). **Heavenly:** a building from God, eternal, not built by human

hands (v 1); our heavenly dwelling (v 2); clothed, life (v 4).

- **According to Paul, which is the better dwelling?** From these descriptions, the heavenly, eternal, and life-filled dwelling— in other words, the heavenly resurrection body—is clearly the better one.

Note: Be aware that many Christians fail to understand that they will receive a physical resurrection body in eternity. They may view eternal life as a purely spiritual existence. This view of eternity is actually closer to Buddhism than the teaching of the Bible. This question is a good opportunity to discuss the reality of our resurrection bodies, and perhaps to begin to correct some of the ideas about our future eternal life that may have come up in Talkabout—floating on clouds, ourselves as disembodied spirits etc. See Romans 8 v 11; 1 Corinthians 15 v 20-23, 42-44; Philippians 3 v 20-21.

3. Why do we groan in this body?
Verses 2-3: Paul longs for his eternal resurrection body because then he will be adequately clothed. **Verse 4:** Paul groans because he feels burdened in his earthly, mortal body. Paul suffered mentally and physically because of his work for the gospel. Our experiences might not match his, and yet we still experience problems with health—mentally and physically, in relationships, in our work and home life, and so on. These are both directly and indirectly the result of sin. And so, in this imperfect body and imperfect world, we groan. See also Romans 8 v 10-11, 18-23.

- **What is it about our earthly bodies that makes us feel naked and burdened? See 4 v 8-12.** "Naked": suggests we feel exposed to both danger

and shame. We feel unprotected. Our bodies themselves give us trouble eg: pain, weariness, increasing disability and lack of dignity as we age, mental fragility, uncontrollable passions and lusts, and constant—and finally inescapable— vulnerability to death. "Burdened": suggests we lack freedom. We are unable to control or escape from the bodily troubles listed above.

- **How will our eternal resurrection bodies be different?** We will feel clothed—not exposed to danger or shame, unburdened and bursting with life.

EXPLORE MORE
- **What does the prophet praise God for in Isaiah 25 v 1-5?** The "wonderful things" he has done (v 1), destroying and subduing the strong (v 2-3, 5) and protecting the weak (v 4).

- **What does the prophet look forward to in v 6-9?** The day when the Lord will reveal himself to all nations on the mountain and prepare a feast for them (v 6-7)—notice the veil/shroud language in v 7. He will defeat and swallow up death, wipe away tears (v 8), and bring salvation (v 9).

- **How does this compare with what Paul waits for?** Paul uses different imagery but he waits for the same thing—the display of God's salvation to all nations, which will lead to our new resurrection bodies, and to the end of groaning and tears. The picture here is different, but complementary.

- **As well as promising salvation, what else is promised in v 10-12?** Judgment will also come. Here in verse 10, judgment is promised against Moab (one of Israel's traditional enemies), but that judgment is an example of a wider judgment, also mentioned in v 1-5.

4. Why is Paul so confident that "what is mortal [will] be swallowed up by life"?
Paul's confidence is based on the promise of God (see Explore More on Isaiah 25 above), and on the guarantee of the Holy Spirit living in us. We can be confident of what is to come because we already have the Spirit within us. You may wish to use the optional extra question if your group have queries about what this means for themselves.

⊽

• **How can a person know if they have the Holy Spirit within them?** The New Testament gives a variety of indicators:

Romans 8 v 15-16: someone who has come to understand that God is their Father.

v 23: someone who is eagerly looking forward to the new creation.

1 Corinthians 2 v 12-14: someone who accepts the gospel.

1 Corinthians 12 v 3: someone who confesses the lordship of Christ.

v 13: someone who lives in unity with other Christians of diverse backgrounds.

Galatians 5 v 16-25: someone who is fighting against what the sinful nature wants and who is growing the fruits of the Spirit—see also Romans 8 v 13.

5. Where would Paul rather be? Why?
Paul would rather be in eternity, with his Lord, because that is his home. This question can be answered fairly simply, but it's another good opportunity to discuss how Paul's view and ours might differ—do we view eternity as our home?

6. APPLY: Christians can be confident of eternal life. How should this make our lives look different from those around us?
This question seeks to underline the fact that confident faith always results in transformed life and behaviour. Encourage your group to think through the implications for themselves and then share them. However, if they are slow to contribute, here are some suggestions: Our priorities will be about things that last for eternity—godliness, the gospel, people and their spiritual needs, the church—rather than things that perish with this world—money, education, career etc. We will "groan" in this present life—we will not expect fulfilment here and now, and will not spend our lives in pursuit of as much as this world can offer. We will be able to persevere and even rejoice in hardship and suffering because our hopes are set on the world to come.

Note: This question raises two slightly different issues—**1.** What are we looking forward to? **2.** How confident are we of that hope? Depending on the people in your group, you may wish to deal with either or both of them.

7. What should be our response to knowing that Christ will judge all of us?
We should seek to please him (v 9) because we will be judged according to what we have done (v 10). Make sure your group rightly understands judgment as an encouragement to rely on Christ (see Summary above and 5 v 21), and not as a reason for doubting our ultimate salvation. Check out Romans 8 v 1-4 if necessary.

Note: If, at this point, some people in your group raise the issue of rewards in heaven, it may be helpful to refer them to some of the New Testament passages that mention this: **The words of Jesus** eg: in the Sermon on the Mount—Matthew 6, see v 1, 4, 6, 18; **the words of Paul**—1 Corinthians 3 v 10-15; Ephesians 6 v 7-8; Colossians 3 v 23-24; **the words of Jesus in Revelation**—Revelation 22 v 11-12. Notice that in each of these passages, rewards are mentioned as an incentive to persevere in living out the Christian faith.

8. As followers of Jesus Christ, what will happen to us when we die? An opportunity to summarise. We will face judgment, but Christ our Judge is also our Saviour, and has already paid the penalty for our sins on the cross (2 Corinthians 5 v 21; Romans 8 v 1-4). We will receive a new body—heavenly, eternal, and made by God. And we will finally be at home in the new heaven and earth with Jesus.

9. APPLY: How does our attitude to eternity sometimes differ from Paul's? Why? It may be helpful to review what was said in answer to question 1 if the views expressed there were significantly different from Paul's view of eternal life. Otherwise encourage your group to talk about the kinds of pressures and temptations that can make our eternal future seem less attractive. The reason for Paul's confidence and anticipation is that he lives by faith and not by sight (v 7). Emphasise here the need to see things rightly as Paul sees them ie: to live by faith, not by sight. It is when we live by sight and not by faith that our attitude begins to differ from his.

• **What have we learned that will help us keep a right view of our eternal lives?** We need to use what we have learned from this passage to correct

misconceptions, and then to live out our faith by seeking to please the Lord as we look forward to eternal life.

10. APPLY: How can we go wrong in our attitude to God's judgment? Why does this happen? There are two main errors we can fall into with regard to God's judgment. **1.** We don't take it seriously. By contrast, Paul's view of God's judgment shapes how he lives his whole life—his goal is to please the Lord because he knows we must all stand before the judgment seat of Christ (v 9-10). **2.** We live in great fear of God's judgment. Paul, however, is confident and longing to be with the Lord (v 8). He looks forward to his new resurrection body. He can be confident in the face of God's judgment because he relies on Christ alone (v 21).

There are a couple of reasons why we can go wrong in our attitude to God's judgment. We may ignore it or minimise it because that makes life easier when we are surrounded by people who hate and oppose the idea of God's judgment. Or we have a wrong view of God's character, believing that he is loving and merciful but disregarding the fact that he is holy and just. We may fear God's judgment because we have never properly understood the gospel of God's grace to undeserving sinners and Christ's sacrifice in our place. Again, we can have a wrong view of God's character, believing that he is holy and just, but unable to accept that he is loving and gracious.

• **What have we learned that will help us keep a right view of God's judgment?** Use what has been learned in the session to (gently) correct people's misconceptions.

7

2 Corinthians 5 v 11-21
LIFE AND DEATH
Why we share the gospel

THE BIG IDEA
Christ's love compels us to share the gospel of Jesus Christ—so this is what a true disciple of Christ will seek to do.

SUMMARY
Again, don't lose the links between this passage and what comes before it: chapter 4 v 1-6 has mentioned the need to share the gospel without losing heart, and 5 v 9-10 gives the immediate context—of sharing Christ in the light of the coming judgment. Paul himself explicitly makes this connection in verse 11.

Paul wants the Corinthians to learn from his example—why, despite the persecution and suffering it causes him, he shares the good news: because he is compelled by the love of Christ—by what Christ has done for him and us (v 15). At the same time, he wants them to see that all Christians are given this calling to be ministers of reconciliation (it is those who are reconciled who have the ministry of reconciliation, v 18). He also wants the Corinthians (and us) to know what to say, and so, from verse 14 onwards, the gospel is summarised in various overlapping ways. Paul tells us to speak in the light of what is to come, and tells us what we need to say.

OPTIONAL EXTRA
You could use this activity in conjunction with question 6 or question 11.

1. If you feel that your group is inexperienced in sharing the gospel, find a simple but memorable gospel summary that you have used with non-Christians and teach it to your group, perhaps at the end of the session. Encourage them to memorise it and give time for a brief reminder and practice at the beginning of the next session.

2. If you feel that there are people in your group who are experienced at sharing the gospel, ask them to share one summary or illustration they have found really helpful (you may need to ask them in advance of the session).

GUIDANCE ON QUESTIONS
Note: Before looking at the questions— a note on timekeeping! There are two "talkabout" sections this session (questions 1 and 6), so be aware of the time you are spending on each one.

1. Think about something you're known for talking constantly about. Why do you want so much to share that discovery or insight with others? Usually it's not hard to find examples of people who can't stop talking about their favourite sports team or band, or someone who is always recommending, say, a particular diet or cold remedy. If no one in your group owns up to this kind of enthusiasm or hobby-horse, get them to think of people they know who are like this. We share our enthusiasms with others because part of the enjoyment of something comes from telling people about it. CS Lewis observed that: "just as men spontaneously praise whatever they value, so they spontaneously urge us to join them in praising it. 'Isn't she lovely? Wasn't it glorious? Don't you think that magnificent?'" Or we may go on about something because we are convinced that it is good for people and we feel responsible for their wellbeing. The aim of this question is to prepare the ground for comparing our enthusiasm and sense of responsibility for telling people the gospel.

As the theme of this session is sharing the gospel, if you know that people in your group do this or try to do it, you could ask them the following question:

⊻

• **Think of a time when you shared the gospel with someone, or tried to. What were your reasons for doing that?** There might be a variety of reasons for sharing the gospel. We might think in terms of people wanting to enjoy what we have as followers of Jesus; we may share the gospel because people ask us; we may do it because we know we should; we may want to impress other Christians; some may enjoy being different and counter-cultural. Some of these reasons are better ones than others. You may wish to list them on a flipchart. As you go through the session, God's word should refocus us on the best reasons why we share the gospel.

2. Why does Paul share the gospel, even when this causes him suffering? Because he knows what is to come—resurrection and judgment—and he fears the Lord. He does not want others to face God's wrath, and he is conscious of his own responsibility to share the good news.

3. What is Paul's attitude to what others think of him? Make sure that your group first understand what some of the Corinthians thought of Paul. Use the

following question if you wish, or outline the answer given.

⊻

• **What do people think of Paul?** There are indications throughout this letter that Paul's apostleship was despised by some of the Corinthians, in part because he was suffering persecution as a result of his ministry. In 1 v 1-11 he has explained why God allows one of his apostles to suffer, and again in 4 v 7-18. Here, in 5 v 11-14, he wants the Corinthians to answer those who take pride in appearances, presumably of power, success and influence, and who have no time for an apparently weak, unimpressive apostle like Paul. Later in the letter, it's clear that some Corinthian "super-apostles" were spuriously claiming their ministry was superior to Paul's (11 v 5), so he sets out to show them up (11 v 16-33), by superficially adopting their worldly strategy of boasting, but subverting it to boast about something that the super-apostles would never have boasted in—his suffering and "the things that show my weakness" (v 30), things that also reveal Christ's power at work in him.

Paul is not commending, or proving, himself to the Corinthians again, since they already know him, and so, in fact, they should be boasting in him and in his willingness to suffer for the gospel, because, despite the appearance of weakness, that is of much greater value than the outward appearance of others who just seem impressive (v 12). As we saw in 2 v 17 – 3 v 1, Paul's main concern here (v 11) is for what God thinks of him, and not for what his opponents think of him. But he is hopeful that his readers, as

Christians under his care, will come to see him as God sees him.

Note: Verse 13—from the context, it seems that "out of [his] mind" is a slander perpetrated by those who despise Paul's ministry, probably for what they believe to be his "mad fanaticism" in keeping on with his gospel ministry even though it constantly provokes persecution against him. True to his principle of acting with sincerity before God rather than labouring to commend himself to others, Paul refrains from refuting the slander in detail. Instead, he simply replies that, if his readers judge that he is out of his mind, then they can trust that some mysterious purpose of God will be furthered by it. But if his readers judge that actually Paul is in his right mind, then they should also conclude that it is for their benefit that Paul continues in both his ministry and suffering.

4. Why is Paul compelled by Christ's love? An opportunity to review the heart of the gospel message. Christ's love is revealed in him dying for all. Because Christ died on the cross on our behalf for the things we have done wrong, those who are in Christ have also died—they have died to selfish living. And just as Christ was raised again, Christians are raised to a new life of living for the Lord, and so must respond to Christ's call to share the good news. Notice that Paul is "convinced" about the significance and implications of Christ's death. There is a clear link between his conviction and the fact that he is compelled by Christ's love to share the gospel.

- **What does the word "compel" tell us?** If you are compelled, you have no choice. You could get people to compare other situations in which they have been or felt compelled to do something, and then ask if they have ever felt similarly about sharing the gospel.

5. APPLY: How do our reasons for sharing the good news with others compare with Paul's? At this point, you could return to the list of reasons written up in answer to question 1 above, and compare them with what Paul says in v 14-15. Our motivation should not be that of duty or seeking to earn God's favour or looking good in church. It is the love that Christ has shown us that should motivate us to long earnestly to share him with others, knowing that judgment is coming. Nor should we view it as an optional extra for the super-committed or particularly gifted Christians in our church, or something for when we feel like it or have the time. Rather, this is something that we have no choice but to get involved with, regardless of the consequences.

- **Why are our attitude and motivation sometimes so different from Paul's?** By comparing themselves with Paul, your group should be able to highlight some of the reasons why Christians today share the gospel for wrong reasons or why they do not feel compelled to share it. These include: not truly understanding the gospel and the extent of Christ's love for us; concern about opponents of the gospel rather than about what God thinks of us; fear of persecution; lack of conviction about the coming judgment, or about our future hope and reward; getting distracted by other activities; failure to understand that we have died to our old selfish way of living etc.

6. If someone asked you to explain the gospel to them, what would you want to say? Encourage people to mention the kind of things they might say. Depending on your group, you could get a few people to give a two-minute summary, or write down for the whole group the various things that people want to mention. If people disagree on what should be included, encourage them to put the discussion on hold until question 11, after you've looked at the rest of the passage.

7. How does Paul describe what Christ has done for us? We are a new creation (v 17); we are reconciled to God (v 18); our sins have been forgiven (v 19); because Christ became sin for us and died on the cross in our place (v 21).

8. Why does Paul regard Christ differently now? Paul's changed heart, because he is a new creation, is responsible for his re-evaluation of Jesus Christ, and therefore he no longer sees Christ from a worldly point of view.

Note: Make sure that your group are aware of the implications of Paul's statement here. Becoming a Christian is not just about intellectually accepting the Bible's view of Jesus Christ, nor about turning over a new leaf and sorting out your life. It is nothing less than a miracle of God, re-creating us and giving us true life for the first time in our human existence. See John 1 v 12-13 and the words of Jesus in John 3 v 3-6.

• **What constitutes a worldly view of Jesus, and how should a Christian view him differently?** Encourage your group to work out the answer to this question from Paul's "new creation" view of Christ set out in these verses. Anything that departs from this is a worldly view of Jesus.

9. What has God made all those who are reconciled to God? All Christians have been reconciled to God through Christ; therefore, all Christians have been made ministers of reconciliation and ambassadors for Christ, with a message to proclaim. As ambassadors and ministers we serve God faithfully in the ministry He has given to us.

Note: Be aware that some people equate the words "minister" and "ministry" with paid employees of the church, and may be surprised that all Christians, not just church leaders, are ministers—in which case, Paul's words here will have profound implications for their view of church and the part they should play in its activities.

10. Look at Paul's explanation of the good news he proclaimed. Complete the table and then summarise the message.

Christ	Us
(v 10) Christ will judge us all	(v 10) We are all going to be judged by Christ
(v 14) Christ died for all	(v 15) In Christ, we no longer live for ourselves but for him
(v 15) Christ was raised again to be Lord	(v 17) In Christ, we are made a new creation

Christ	Us
(v 21) Christ was sinless but was treated as a sinner on our behalf	(v 18) In Christ, we are reconciled to God
	(v 19) In Christ, God doesn't count our sins against us
	(v 21) In Christ, we who are sinners can be given the righteousness of God

The summary will depend on who is in your group, but you would expect it to include:

• We are all deserving of God's judgment (5 v 10-11).

• Christ died for us on the cross, taking the punishment we deserve, so that we might live (5 v 14-15).

• In Christ, we are a new creation (v 17), reconciled to God (v 18), and forgiven of our sins (v 19), because Christ became sin for us and died on the cross in our place (v 21).

11. APPLY: This is an opportunity to encourage people (especially if they have never shared the gospel before) with a variety of practical ideas and suggestions. (See Optional Extra.)

How should our lives be affected by the truth that...

a. we have a message of reconciliation?
We need to think about how we show people both that they need to be reconciled (without Christ they are enemies of God) and that God wants all people to be reconciled to him. Questions to consider may include: Do we skip bits about sin and judgment when we talk to people about God? Do we give an impression that God is either soft on sin or petty, mean, ungracious etc? How do we show that reconciliation is important in the way we live?

b. we are ambassadors of Christ? Just like a national ambassador, as ambassadors for Christ we are on duty the whole time. Anything that we say or do will reflect on Christ. You could ask people to share what it will mean for them to represent Christ to the world 24/7.

c. we have good news to proclaim?
Being a minister of reconciliation and an ambassador for Christ means being involved in the proclamation of the Christian message. Non-Christians need to hear the words of the gospel message as well as seeing the lives of those saved by the gospel. Of course, not everyone is gifted to speak in public. The key point is that we should be helping people to hear the gospel. Get your group to think about the various ways in which we can do that—giving a tract, bringing someone to hear a gospel presentation, sharing your testimony in a private conversation, writing a letter, inviting and taking someone to a course that introduces the gospel etc.

8
2 Corinthians 6 v 1 – 7 v 1
GRACE, NOT STUMBLING BLOCKS   Helping and being helped

THE BIG IDEA
True disciples of Christ will receive God's grace by repenting when they are challenged by God's word.

SUMMARY
Paul has given a long defence of his conduct as an apostle, and his motives for doing what he did. In chapters 6 and 7 he draws this part of the letter to its climax. Here in chapter 6, he reminds the Corinthians of God's grace and his own sufferings, before warning them about their conduct. We'll look first at 6 v 1-13, before looking at 6 v 14 – 7 v 1 (and then coming back to look again at 6 v 1-2).

The Corinthians need to take the opportunity to repent now (6 v 1-2). Paul warns them that the opportunity will not last for ever.

The Corinthians have seen Paul's conduct among them. He is confident that he has not put any stumbling block in their way. They need to reflect on what they know of him, and must listen to him, even when he says something that they don't like. He isn't hurting them by speaking in this way—but they are restricting their affections by not responding to God's word (v 3-13).

So the Corinthians need to separate from unbelievers (6 v 14 – 7 v 1). That is the thrust of the two Old Testament quotations here, which both deal with Israel being a special, holy people, separate from the other nations. It is also the thrust of the call to be cleansed in 7 v 1. What does this

separation mean? In parallel with Israel in the land of Canaan (see Leviticus 26), it means not getting involved in relationships which will draw us away from the Lord and into worldly conduct—into being ruled by the world. This has obvious implications for marriage, but also for some business relationships and other contracts that we might enter into, as well as more mundane things like who we have as friends.

OPTIONAL EXTRA
1. (For younger or more active groups) Divide your group into pairs, or select four people to make two pairs. Try to ensure that one of your pairs is unequal eg: the largest person in your group paired with the smallest. Make sure your pairs are linked eg: bound to each other by one ankle as in a three-legged race. Then give the pairs a route to complete, either against the clock or in a race with another pair. The classic three-legged race is simplest if you have access to space, or you could get them to move around your venue in a way that involves overcoming obstacles eg: up and down stairs, under a table, over a sofa etc. The pairs that are similar should be more successful. The main practical challenge of this session is about Christians being unequally yoked with non-Christians.

2. (For all the rest—as an extension to question 1) Give your group one or more of the following situations: a marriage between a Christian and a follower of another religion; a business partnership between a Christian and a non-Christian; a community project organised between a Bible-teaching church and a liberal church; a Christian teacher in an explicitly multi-faith school; a Christian politician in a secular government. Ask people to identify the kinds of problems for a Christian in these situations.

GUIDANCE ON QUESTIONS

Note: The two Explore More questions can be treated separately, and just one selected if there is not enough time to do both.

1. How close should Christians get in their relationships with unbelievers? At this stage, the purpose of this question is to see how people think about engaging with the world. So, some might be negative about doing anything with people who aren't Christians—others may be more positive about engagement. This discussion should open up the way for all to be challenged by what Paul has to say here.

2. What do the Corinthians need to do? When and why? The Corinthians need to ensure that they are not receiving the grace of God in vain. They need to do this now, because the implication of verse 2 is that there is a limited time available. The rest of this chapter will expand on what it means for the Corinthians not to receive the grace of God in vain.

3. Paul commends himself to the Corinthians as a servant of God. How will this help them to receive God's grace? God's grace is coming to the Corinthians at this time through the ministry of Paul. But if they doubt that Paul is a true servant of God, they will not listen to him. (Remember that Paul's apostleship was under attack from some in Corinth.) So Paul sets out to show that he is a true apostle of

Christ and to remove any "stumbling block" that would hinder the Corinthians from receiving God's grace.

4. How does Paul commend himself to the Corinthians? Paul and those with him commend themselves in a number of ways:

a. in their willingness to undergo suffering for the gospel (v 4-5)

b. in how they live their lives—in a godly way, being loving and speaking truth (v 6-7)

c. in continuing to be faithful despite what others say (v 8)

d. in all situations—by being focused on what Christ has done (v 8-10, compare 4 v 10-11)

Paul places no stumbling block (v 3) in the way of the Corinthians receiving God's grace from him, because he seeks to act in a godly manner at all times, even in hardship and suffering.

Note: Previously in this letter, Paul has shown some reluctance to commend himself to the Corinthians eg: 3 v 1 and 5 v 12. The reason for this is that it was a characteristic of his opponents, the "super-apostles", who so looked down on Paul and his apostleship—boasting about themselves was part of their stock-in-trade for promoting their so-called ministry. Paul's attitude is that he does not need to commend himself because the Lord will commend him (10 v 18). If he is to commend himself in any way, it will be by setting out the truth about himself before men's consciences (4 v 2), which means pointing out the very things that cause his opponents to denounce him as a servant of God—his hardships and suffering for the gospel.

5. What does Paul want the Corinthians to do? To open their hearts to him. This will involve a closer personal relationship with Paul, but more than that...

6. What will this mean for the Corinthians, in the light of verse 1? It will also involve listening to and responding to what he has to say—they need to open their hearts to Paul, and God's message through him, however hard it is for them to hear.

7. APPLY: How can we follow Paul's example and not put stumbling blocks in the way of people hearing God's message? Both questions 7 and 8 deal with specifics, and therefore the areas of our own conduct—in speaking or listening—that we need to work on will be different. To get the discussion going in a direction related to the Bible passage, you could first of all go through the list of characteristics in v 4-10 that commend Paul as a true servant of God, and work out the opposites. You will then have a list of behaviours that are likely to put stumbling blocks in the way of people who need to hear the gospel from you.

The list includes: giving up easily, opting for comfort, avoiding hardship, laziness, lack of commitment (v 4-5), impurity, ignorance, impatience, unkindness, acting in our own strength, attempting to appear loving without really being so (v 6), using deceptive and lying words, failing to rely on God's power, lacking righteousness (v 7), being fair-weather Christians (v 8-9), people who don't rejoice, don't make others rich, and don't revel in the treasures that are ours in Christ. Challenge your group to think about which of these failings they might be prone to, and what they need to do to remove these stumbling blocks.

8. APPLY: How can we avoid being like the Corinthians who won't listen to Paul? Briefly recap the reasons we have come across so far as to why the Corinthians might have decided not listen to Paul—because he suffers for the gospel (1 v 3-11); because he changed his plans to visit them (1 v 15 – 2 v 2); because he has made a painful visit to them in the past and has had to say some hard things to them (2 v 1, 4, 9); because, unlike others, he does not profit from God's word or carry around letters of recommendation (2 v 17 – 3 v 3); because some accuse him of being out of his mind (5 v 13). Challenge your group to reflect on whether they have ever used reasons like these as justification for not listening to a Christian leader.

9. What reasons does Paul give for not being "yoked" to an unbeliever? Paul likens close relationships between believers and unbelievers to the following contrasts: righteousness/unrighteousness, light/darkness, Christ/Belial, and the temple of God/idols. The fact that these are such extreme opposites forces us to the conclusion that unbelievers and believers cannot ever be yoked together. Paul justifies this by identifying believers as the temple of God, because God dwells among his people (v16)—this means that those among whom God dwells must be separate from the people around them, so as not to be polluted by the world.

10. What does it mean to be yoked to an unbeliever? As we look at the reasons for not being yoked, we also see what it means to be yoked. An unequal yoke is any situation where serving another human being who is not a Christian results in a Christian being compromised in their ability to serve and worship God. So, business and work situations might qualify—but don't necessarily. So too with friendships. However, the closer the yoking, the more likely it is that a problem will result, and therefore it is no surprise that one of the primary applications of this passage is in relation to marriage.

EXPLORE MORE

Leviticus 26 v 1-13: Why do you think Paul quotes from this passage? This is about the blessings that God's people, Israel, would enjoy in the promised land if they remained obedient to God, who brought them out of Egypt. God had broken the yoke of the Egyptians (v 13) and had made Israel into his people. Since Israel were now God's people, they were not to make themselves slaves again, by being unequally yoked to anyone else.

What are the parallels between Israel then and Christians now? Like Israel, Christians have been rescued from slavery—to sin and death—by the mighty work of God, through the sacrifice of his Son on the cross. Those saved by Jesus Christ join the church, which is now the people of God, and which, like Israel, is being taken to the promised land—eternal life in the new heaven and earth. If God commanded his people to be set apart for him under the old covenant with Israel, how much more should Christians live lives of separated purity for their Lord under the greater promises of the new covenant through Christ.

Isaiah 52 v 1-12: What is happening in this passage (compare Isaiah 48 v 20), and how does it help Paul to make his point? Where Leviticus 26 tells us about Israel after the exodus from Egypt, Isaiah 52 prophesies the restoration and cleansing of Jerusalem after God's people have spent 70 years of exile in Babylon (v 1-2). God speaks

of the future—as he has in the past—and brings news of the restoration of Zion, and the Lord's return there (v 3-8). This prophecy resulted in the restoration of Judah, the faithful remnant of Israel, but also promises a more universal salvation (v 9-10), that is being fulfilled today in Jesus Christ and his gospel to all nations. When the exiles returned to Jerusalem, they carried with them vessels of the temple that were needed for the worship of God in the temple of Jerusalem. Those who carried the vessels needed to be clean and separate, as people dedicated to the Lord (v11-12).
Parallel today: Similarly, Christians today have been rescued from their exile from God. Uniquely among all the people on the earth, Christians can now serve and worship the one true God, and need to be pure and uncontaminated as they do this.

11. Look at what Paul says in 7 v 1. How does this relate to what he has said in 6 v 1? In 6 v 1 Paul says don't receive the grace of God in vain. In 7 v 1 he says be cleansed and be holy. Given what he says in between about listening to God's word through him (v 3-13) and being unequally yoked (v 14-18), it would seem that the Corinthians, or at least some of them, were disregarding God's grace by their unwillingness to obey God's word and their failure to seek to live holy lives.

12. APPLY: How are we in danger of being unequally yoked with unbelievers? What are we going to do about it? This will vary according to the people in your group. It is quite possible that this Bible passage will open up uncomfortable questions for some people in the group, in relation to their family and/or business relationships. By all means discuss those a little, but it may be wise to involve your church leaders (make sure you don't break any confidences), as many of these issues involve not just understanding what God's word says, but also how that can be worked out in ongoing situations.

PRAY
Be sure to pray for anyone who is struggling with these issues, as well as those things mentioned in the Study Guide.

---

2 Corinthians 7 v 2-16
DISCIPLINE AND ENCOURAGEMENT
Responding to godly correction

THE BIG IDEA
True disciples will respond in the right way to godly correction.

SUMMARY
This chapter can be a little hard to follow—we need to remember what has gone before, and to read slowly and carefully.

Paul begins in 7 v 2 with an appeal; it's the same appeal as in 6 v 11. Paul wants the Corinthians to listen to him, and is confident that they should, because of his conduct before them, and because of his care for and love of them (v 2-4).

He talks again about how he and his colleagues had no rest when they first came into Macedonia, until Titus came and comforted Paul with news of the Corinthians and how they had repented (v 5-7). These verses pick up the story of their journey mentioned in 2 v 12-13. There, Paul left Troas and went to Macedonia because he didn't find Titus. Here, he meets with Titus in Macedonia, and is comforted. He has been fearful about the Corinthians, and how they would respond to what he has

said, and isn't comforted until Titus arrives with some good news.

And so although he didn't wish to grieve them, Paul is happy that they have responded to his words with godly grief, and with repentance—and have punished the wrongdoer (v 8-11). Remember that back in 2 Corinthians 2 v 5-11, Paul was encouraging them to forgive the repentant wrongdoer—they had clearly responded, with some zeal, to his request (2 v 6). Then Paul points out that when he wrote, it was for the sake of the Corinthians, and so their response has comforted him (7 v 12-13). Titus has also been encouraged by their response, and his affection for them has increased (v 13-15). And, as Paul reminds them in verse 16, whatever he has to say to the Corinthians, he has confidence in them.

On a practical level, this session challenges us with both the example of Paul, in his deep love for the Corinthian Christians, and the example of the Corinthians, in their godly response to Paul's painful correction and their willingness to grow as true disciples of Jesus Christ.

OPTIONAL EXTRA

Divide your group into teams. One member of each team is blindfolded and given a task to do eg: complete an obstacle course, make a sandwich, draw a route on a map etc. The rest of the team give instructions. This activity will work even better if you get two teams to compete against each other at the same time. Listen out for, and then comment on, how team members correct and encourage their representative. This can then be compared later in the session with the way in which Paul goes about correcting the Corinthians (see questions 2, 5 and 9).

GUIDANCE ON QUESTIONS

1. Have you ever been corrected by a church leader or fellow Christian? How did you respond? No doubt (hopefully) everyone will have had some experience of being challenged and corrected by a church leader or a more mature Christian. It is rarely a comfortable process, and if we've been Christians for some time, we can probably all look back on times when we have not responded well to what was being said. This question should at least highlight both the importance of correction (ie: discipline or challenge) and the question of how we respond. It is possible that some will reject the idea of discipline as either un-Christian or outmoded. Chapter 7 of 2 Corinthians will demonstrate that it is neither. One issue that may affect our response to correction is where there is a poor quality of relationship between the Christians involved, and this issue is also addressed in the session.

2. Why does Paul want the Corinthians to make room in their hearts for him? As in chapter 6, Paul wants them to listen to him, and he cares deeply for them—how they respond to him will affect him personally, bringing either grief or comfort.

• **How deep are Paul's feelings for the Corinthian Christians?** Great commitment—he would die for them (v 3); great confidence, great pride, great encouragement and great joy (v 4).

3. Who comforts Paul, and who comforts Titus here? Titus comforts Paul by the good news he brings. The Corinthians comfort Titus by their zeal and repentance. At the same time, notice how Paul recognises that it is God who comforts him, through Titus.

4. APPLY: Think about the depths of Paul's feelings for the Corinthian Christians. How do your relationships with fellow believers in your church compare? Concern about the Corinthian Christians caused Paul and his colleagues to be restless, anxious and downcast (v 5-6). Good news gave them great joy, confidence, pride and encouragement (v 4, 7). But our relationships with fellow Christians in our church, apart from a few close friends, may be more like those of acquaintances than the intense love that Paul shows here. In other words, they are people with whom we can enjoy chit-chat over a cup of coffee after the Sunday service, but may barely remember for the rest of the week. It may be helpful to ask your group to reflect on the following questions:

• When was the last time you found it difficult to sleep because of concern for a fellow Christian?

• When was the last time you were moved to tears of compassion by the predicament or failing of a fellow Christian?

- When was the last time you were so full of joy and pride at the godliness of a fellow Christian that you had to share it with someone else?

- When was the last time you pestered someone for news about a fellow Christian that you were concerned about, and couldn't relax until you'd heard about them?

- When was the last time that you chose to initiate a difficult conversation or wrote a difficult letter to a Christian because you were concerned about them?

- When was the last time you made a commitment to pray daily for a fellow Christian and carried it through?

- **What can you do to become more like Paul? (Note:** Remember that it is only because of the gospel that we have anything at all in common with some Christians. Ultimately it is understanding, living and working for the gospel that draws us into unity with Christian brothers and sisters.) Get the group to share ideas that they can put into practice in the coming weeks. A prayer list of names from your church would be a good place to start and could involve seeking people out and asking what you could pray for them, and then following that up later. Involvement in serving the church is a good way to get to know people better. Hospitality is something that most can do, even if it's just tea and biscuits. Use the time you spend with people to find out how they became a Christian—it's a good way of moving on from mere social chit-chat. After each Sunday meeting, aim to speak to one person about what you have been learning or doing together.

5. Look at the news Paul receives. What is it that makes him rejoice? Paul doesn't rejoice in grieving the Corinthians, but he does rejoice that they have responded well, and have repented, thus demonstrating godly sorrow.

6. What is the difference between godly and worldly sorrow? Godly sorrow is grief at one's actions that leads to repentance before the Lord, and therefore forgiveness and salvation. Worldly sorrow leads to death because there is no repentance—only either sorrow at being found out, or grief at being criticised.

EXPLORE MORE
In Revelation 18 we read of the fall of the great city, Babylon, and how people mourn for her. What does worldly grief look like? Revelation 18 gives us a picture of various people who have suffered from the fall of Babylon—the kings who have consorted with her and the merchants who have made themselves rich from trading with her (notice how the cargo list includes slaves, v 13). They are not repenting when they see Babylon's fate: they are lamenting that they will no longer be able to benefit from her. Worldly sorrow is ultimately selfish—things that go wrong are evaluated only in the light of how they affect us.

7. Who has benefitted from the sending of the letter mentioned here? And how have they benefitted? The Corinthians have benefitted, revealed by their earnestness toward God (v 11). Paul has benefitted because their actions have comforted him (v 13), and Titus has benefitted (v 13-15) because he has seen the repentance and zeal of the Corinthians in action.

8. Paul talks of his pride in the Corinthians and his boasting about them. What does he boast in? Paul is able to boast about a church that exists in Corinth because God has called it in to being. He boasts about the fact that people have repented and turned to the Lord, and here, about their willingness to repent when they heard God's word. The Corinthians are not a perfect church—neither are they, at least in Paul's eyes, entirely without virtue. (**Note:** Here "boast" = publicly to take delight and pride in something—actually something that God is doing—rather than drawing attention to your own strengths and successes.)

9. Paul has had to say some hard things to the Corinthians. Apart from being an apostle, what gave him the right to say these things? Paul shows here, and throughout this letter, his love for the Corinthians. He doesn't want to hurt them—he wants to be able to boast in them. He loves them, so when he has to say hard things to them, he is unsettled until he hears about their response (here and 2 Corinthians 2). He is confident in his conduct before them, and his conduct before them gives him the right to challenge their behaviour. The best correction comes in the context of a pre-existing relationship of brotherly love.

10. APPLY: From what we have read here, what is the right response to legitimate correction? First of all, we need to make sure correction is legitimate ie: it comes from God's word. Then we need to accept it, which involves praying about it, repenting and asking for God's forgiveness, and finally, seeking by God's grace to change how we live.

11. APPLY: How can we be ready to accept legitimate correction? To be able to accept correction, we need to be those who want to hear God's word, and who are ready to listen to those who would challenge and even criticise us, determined to weigh their words before the Lord, to pray, and to change where necessary. To grow in true discipleship like this, we need to come to know better and better the Lord we follow.

GETTING PERSONAL: This should provoke quite a personal response, and if you have time, you may wish to recap some of the things we have learned from the letter so far. People may not wish to share this, but encourage them to write it down or share it with one other person, and then pray.

A selection from the Good Book Guide series...

1 Thessalonians: Living to Please God *by Mark Wallace*
7 studies. ISBN: 9781904889953

1 John: How to be Sure *by Tim Chester*
7 studies. ISBN: 9781904889953

OLD TESTAMENT

NEW! Judges: The Flawed and the Flawless *by Timothy Keller*
studies. ISBN: 9781908762887

Esther: Royal Rescue *by Jane McNabb*
7 studies. ISBN: 9781908317926

1 Kings 1 – 11: The Rise and Fall of King Solomon *by James Hughes*
8 studies. ISBN: 9781907377976

Jonah: The Depths of Grace *by Stephen Witmer*
6 studies. ISBN: 9781907377433

Hosea: God's Love Song *by Dan Wells*
8 studies. ISBN: 9781905564255

NEW TESTAMENT

Mark 1 – 8: The Coming King *by Tim Chester*
10 studies. ISBN: 9781904889281

1 Corinthians 10 – 16: Challenging Church *by Mark Dever*   7 studies.
ISBN: 9781908317506 (UK) ...681 (US)

Galatians: Gospel Matters *by Timothy Keller*   7 studies.
ISBN: 9781907622559 (UK) ...566 (US)

TOPICAL

Promises Kept (Bible overview) *by Carl Laferton*
9 studies. ISBN: 9781908317933

Biblical Womanhood *by Sarah Young*
10 studies. ISBN: 9781904889076

NEW! Making Work Work *by Marcus Nodder*
8 studies. ISBN: 9781908762894

Experiencing God *by Tim Chester*
6 studies. ISBN: 9781906334437

NEW! Passion: Luke 22 – 24 *by Mike McKinley*
6 studies. ISBN: 9781909559165

Contentment: Healing the Hunger of our Hearts *by Anne Woodcock*
6 studies. ISBN: 9781905564668

Visit your friendly neighbourhood website to see the full range, and to download samples
**USA & Canada: www.thegoodbook.com • UK & Europe: www.thegoodbook.co.uk
Australia: www.thegoodbook.com.au • New Zealand: www.thegoodbook.co.nz**

thegoodbook
COMPANY
Opening up the Bible

At The Good Book Company, we are dedicated to helping Christians and local churches grow. We believe that God's growth process always starts with hearing clearly what he has said to us through his timeless word—the Bible.

Ever since we opened our doors in 1991, we have been striving to produce resources that honour God in the way the Bible is used. We have grown to become an international provider of user-friendly resources to the Christian community, with believers of all backgrounds and denominations using our Bible studies, books, evangelistic resources, DVD-based courses and training events.

We want to equip ordinary Christians to live for Christ day by day, and churches to grow in their knowledge of God, their love for one another, and the effectiveness of their outreach.

Call us for a discussion of your needs or visit one of our local websites for more information on the resources and services we provide.

UK & Europe: www.thegoodbook.co.uk
North America: www.thegoodbook.com
Australia: www.thegoodbook.com.au
New Zealand: www.thegoodbook.co.nz

UK & Europe: 0333 123 0880
North America: 866 244 2165
Australia: (02) 6100 4211
New Zealand (+64) 3 343 1990

www.christianityexplored.org

Our partner site is a great place for those exploring the Christian faith, with a clear explanation of the good news, powerful testimonies and answers to difficult questions.

One life. What's it all about?